# THE SPANISH LEGAL TRADITION

# The Spanish Legal Tradition

An Introduction to the Spanish Law and Legal System

CHARLOTTE VILLIERS
*University of Glasgow*

**Ashgate**

DARTMOUTH

Aldershot • Brookfield USA • Singapore • Sydney

Published by
Dartmouth Publishing Company Ltd
Ashgate Publishing Ltd
Gower House
Croft Road
Aldershot
Hants GU11 3HR
England

Ashgate Publishing Company
Old Post Road
Brookfield
Vermont 05036
USA

**British Library Cataloguing in Publication Data**
Villiers, Charlotte
    The Spanish legal tradition : an introduction to the
    Spanish law and legal system. – (Laws of the nations
    series)
    1.Law – Spain
    I.Title
    349.4'6

**Library of Congress Cataloging-in-Publication Data**
Villiers, Charlotte.
    The Spanish legal tradition : an introduction to the Spanish law
    and legal system / Charlotte Villiers.
        p.  cm.
    ISBN 1-85521-852-6 (hb)
    1. Law—Spain.   I. Title.
KKT68.V55   1999
349.46—dc21                                                        98-52036
                                                                        CIP

ISBN 1 85521 852 6 (HBK)
      0 7546 2099 9 (PBK)

Typeset by Manton Typesetters, 5–7 Eastfield Road, Louth, Lincs, LN11 7AJ, UK.

Printed and bound by Athenaeum Press, Ltd., Gateshead, Tyne & Wear.

# Contents

# Preface

Compared with the legal systems of some other European Union member states, little has been written in the UK about the Spanish law and legal system. Yet, with her unique system of autonomous communities, Spain has much to offer to legal scholars in the UK which now has a devolved Scottish Parliament and regional assemblies for Wales and Northern Ireland.

Increasingly, students are following exchange programmes in Spain and often they go to Spain with little background knowledge of the legal system which they will be going to study. This book seeks primarily to provide such students with an introduction to that law and legal system. It also seeks to introduce comparative lawyers to Spanish law and to provide them with a starting point for their research.

The central focus of the book is the Spanish Constitution of 1978. The constitutional history offers an insight to the Spanish legal and political tradition. The negotiations for and contents of the 1978 constitution also demonstrate Spain's progress towards democracy and political pluralism. Fundamentally for lawyers, the constitution is regarded as the primary source in the hierarchy of laws within the Spanish legal system. Thus a lack of knowledge of the constitution would lead to a lack of understanding of many of the more specific areas of Spanish law. Another key focus of the book is that of the autonomous communities and how the regional state is structured. This may provide points of comparison for current developments in the UK's regional structure. Finally, Spain's relationship with the European Union is worthy of attention, since that is likely to be a leading influence in the future development of a number of Spanish laws.

I wish to thank a number of people without whose generosity this book would not have been completed: the Nuffield Foundation, whose funding (ref: SOC (100)974) enabled me to obtain my Spanish law materials; my publishers, Ashgate Publishing Limited, especially John Irwin and Valerie Saunders for their encouragement and patience; the universities of Oviedo and Jaén in Spain who allowed me access to their law libraries; Peter Luxton, with whom I taught on the Law with Spanish Law Degree in Sheffield and who encouraged me to write the book; Thomas Watkin of

Cardiff University as editor of the series in which this book is written; my Spanish colleagues in Oviedo and Jaén, especially Alicia de León Arce and Gerardo Ruiz-Rico Ruiz with whom I have collaborated in Erasmus and Socrates exchange programmes; and John Brown who gave me the opportunity to visit Jaén. My warmest thanks are due to Tony Prosser, who read and commented on an earlier draft, and gave me heaps of encouragement. Special thanks also go to my students of Spanish law who worked hard without the benefit of an introductory book and with whom I had some very enjoyable discussions, especially Matt Lacey, Tony Theakston, Chris Thornton and Karen Williams.

CHARLOTTE VILLIERS

# 1    Introduction

> Travel for any length of time ... and the sheer variety of this huge country
> cannot fail to impress. The separate kingdoms which made up the original
> Spanish nation remain very much in evidence, in a diversity of language, culture
> and artistic traditions. ... While great monuments still survive from a history
> which takes in Romans, Moors and the 'Golden Age' of Renaissance imperial-
> ism, Spain is breaking out in innumerable – and often unpredictable – ways. The
> sheer pace of change, barrelling into the twentieth century in the wake of the
> thirty-year dictatorship of Generalissimo Franco, is one of the country's most
> stimulating aspects. ... Spain is enjoying the fastest economic growth in Europe,
> and a vitality – revelling in the nation's new-found self-confidence and rediscov-
> ered democracy – which is almost palpable. For the first time in centuries there
> is a feeling of political stability.

This portrayal of Spain, written in the introduction of *Spain: The Rough
Guide*, has relevance not just for holiday travellers to Spain but also for
students of Spanish law. What may be witnessed of Spanish law and culture
is the legacy of almost two centuries of struggle to change Spain from an
isolated and absolutist kingdom to a thriving democracy of the modern
Western world.

Modern Spain prides herself on having established a stable democracy.
The Preamble to the Spanish Constitution of 1978 states that Spain is a
democratic and social state which operates by the rule of law. Spain is a
nation with a key role in international politics and economics and is an
important member of the European Union. Understanding how Spain has
achieved this positive position, both internally and externally, demands at
least a brief tour of her history. In a book about Spanish law it is difficult to
know exactly where to begin. The earliest evidence of laws appears to have
existed with the Iberian tribes. The influence of the Romans as well as the
Visigoths and the Moslems is also apparent. However, this book focuses
primarily on the constitutional aspects of Spanish law, these being one of
the major bases for other specific areas of Spanish law. It may therefore be
appropriate to begin with a history of modern constitutionalism in Spain.

**Historical Aspects**

Today's Spanish Constitution was created in 1978 and is the result mainly of historical and political developments since the nineteenth century. The French Revolution introduced to Spain the concepts of the nation state and political unity. These ideas provided a foundation for the new constitutionalism which highlighted a crisis for Spain's *ancien régime*. A stable constitutional settlement was finally achieved in the late 1970s.

Constitutionalism might be traced back, according to Olivan López *et al.* (1993), as far as the time of the Pharaohs in Ancient Egypt where there was a system of order and institution. The more modern concept, however, has its roots in the political systems of Greece and Rome, but from these times, and for a duration of approximately five centuries, there were divisions between understanding the constitution as being modelled on democracy and aristocracy and between the notion of government by the people and of government by the upper classes. During the Middle Ages, the Magna Carta introduced the notion of the constitution as a guarantee of the rights of citizens against the state. This would later have some influence on Spanish constitutionalism.

*Modern Constitutionalism: the Nineteenth Century*

Spain's constitutional history was influenced by the economic and social conditions of Spain during the nineteenth and twentieth centuries as well by the experiences of other European countries. The period highlights a series of swings from radicalism to moderation and from revolution to restoration of the monarchy. The gradual release from the tyrannical grip of the monarchy did not happen in one step but rather by a pendulum which seemed at times to indicate one progressive step forward and two reactionary steps back.

With the Modern Age there developed the idea of the nation state. As observed by Olivan López *et al.* (1993), the old feudal structure gave way to the state breaking itself away from transnational ties that, during the Middle Ages, had maintained the idea of a common world under the aegis of the empire and the papacy. The new concept of the nation state carved out the beginnings of the idea of political unity. The concept of the nation state arose out of political, economic and social developments leading to philosophies based on rationalism and the separation of powers. The revolutions of France and North America paved the way for the bases of modern constitutionalism. The constitution was endowed with the double characteristic of a unified nation state together with a guarantee of rights and freedoms for citizens. This itself necessitated a form of representative democracy.

The most important periods historically in terms of Spain's modern constitution are the nineteenth and twentieth centuries. During the fifteenth to eighteenth centuries Spain was dominated by a regime of monarchic absolutism which gave strong personal and arbitrary powers to the monarch. Following the Habsburg era, Spain entered into a period of long-term decline under the Bourbons, until Napoleon invaded in 1808.

According to Sánchez Agesta (1980), the nineteenth century and early twentieth century up to the Second Republic (1931–39) may be divided into five different stages: origins of Spanish constitutionalism; constitutional monarchy and middle-class revolution; revolution and restoration of the monarchy; restoration; constitutional crisis. These stages are outlined as follows.

*Origins of Spanish constitutionalism*    Napoleon brought with him to Spain the notion, not of the sovereignty of the king, but of the sovereignty of the nation. The Spanish people attempted to rid themselves of their invader in a war of independence. The old King Fernando VII had gone into exile and the war developed from a defence against the invader into an assault on the previous regime. In 1810, a revolutionary movement established a parliament (the *Cortes*) in Cádiz in which there were representatives from the provinces. This brought about a restructuring of the centralized and unified state headed by the monarch into a new national social structure. The *Cortes* would change from being a body representing a plurality of *estamentos* (local groups) and municipalities and would begin to represent the nation as a whole, as one united entity. A constitution was created in 1812 which lasted until 1820, when Fernando VII returned from exile. This period is characterized by two antagonistic forces: the continuity of Spain's *ancien régime* and nascent constitutionalism – a struggle between the traditional society and a new individualist and egalitarian structure. The privileged groups representing the *ancien régime* included the nobility and the clergy, whereas those demanding equality before the law, freedom of property and freedom of work, together with individual suffrage, were the middle classes. The economic and social climate of this period was different from that of the earlier period.

*The constitutional monarchy and the revolution of the middle classes*    This period marks the reign of Isabel II during which there were formalized many constitutional texts which highlighted the distinctions between the various constitutional solutions proposed by different parties. There were two dominating and opposed lines of thought: one a doctrinaire solution representing a political balance which was reflected by the *Estatuto* (Code) of 1834 and the constitution of 1845; the other a radical or progressive solution highlighted by the constitutions of 1837, 1856 and, especially, the revolutionary constitution of 1869. During this period the middle classes seemed to triumph, the overall result being a compromise between tradition and revolution which would eventually provide the basis of a constitutional monarchy.

*Revolution and restoration of the monarchy*    In 1868, a revolution overthrew the reign of Isabel II and brought to the throne a new king, Amadeo de Saboya, in 1870. This was a period of great unrest. A new constitution was created in 1869 which contained radical provisions, including universal suffrage, for the first time. King Amadeo found it impossible to reign in such an unstable climate. The assassination of General Prim, who had led the revolution and established Amadeo as king, worsened the situation in which there were Cuban, Carlist (those who supported Don Carlos, rival to Isabel II and backed by the Church, Conservatives and Baroques) and republican insurrections, and little support for a foreign king. This context, together with the fact that King Amadeo was a genuine constitutionalist who sought popular endorsement of his position, led him to abdicate the throne in 1873. On the same day the first republic was proclaimed and a draft federal constitution was published. The republican period which followed was itself characterized by a continuing crisis of authority, blighted by both anarchism and federalism, and was therefore shortlived. The monarchy was restored in 1874, when Alfonso XII became king of Spain. This restoration of the monarchy prepared the ground for the constitution of 1876.

*Restoration*    This period was consolidated under the new constitutional text of 1876, which had flexible characteristics arising from its liberal roots. This constitution tried to strike a balance between the middle of the two opposing forces which predated it: the doctrinaire model of 1845 and the radical model of 1869. This constitution sought plural politics under a monarchic constitution and a two-party system seemed to establish itself along the lines of the British Constitution. Both political movements developed formulae which were analogous to those of 1869, such as a right of association and universal suffrage. Socially, the era was characterized by the dominance of the bourgoisie and commercial classes, together with a rise in wealth and the first signs of workers being organized into professional associations. During the reign of Alfonso XII, the death of Canovas and of Sagasta, who led the two main parties, brought about a new type of parliamentary government more comparable in character to the French, with multiple parties and unstable coalitions, which led to the dictatorship of General Primo de Rivera, who took over in 1923. His regime brought about the end of the 1876 constitution and the monarchy.

Throughout the nineteenth century, Spain experienced notable demographic and social changes. As is observed by Sánchez Agesta (1980), the nobility and clergy declined in number and this brought about a change in ownership of property. This in turn helped to establish a new class which obtained political influence. The industrial revolution also made possible the dramatic development of publicity through the introduction of printing and newspapers. Thus Spanish politics, which had previously been characterized by secrecy surrounding the state and government, became more open so that the government was to be a public institution which would be influenced and given legitimacy by the public. This new public life allowed free discussion in the parliament and in the press. Thus, as Sánchez Agesta (ibid.) notes, orators, writers and journalists became very important. Overall, this period marks the rise of the middle classes through new property ownership and the new wealth of speculators and of commercial and industrial actors. These groups controlled the political census so that the right to vote was based on the wealth of the individual.

The period was also dominated by a fluctuation between two contrasting movements: the moderate tradition and the progressive character of Spanish constitutionalism, both of which revolved around the idea of sovereignty, one supporting a moderate sovereign monarchy and the other supporting a progressive people's sovereignty. The moderate movement conceived the unity of the state as a consequence of the unity of the power of the sovereign monarchy. The progressive movement was bound to the popular forces and supported the local autonomies. This movement conceived the unity of the state as a democratic pact between citizens situated across a diversity of towns and regions. The two movements were also contrasted by a distinction between support for a central state and support for a federalist state. Thus the moderate tradition followed the centralizing ideology of the French, while the radicals were bound with federalism typical of the widespread localism of the Spanish. Overall, the moderate tradition enjoyed the longest surviving constitutions. The progressive eras experienced the problem of integrating with their own ideas the conservative interests of the propertied classes who had most real power.

The result of these consistently opposed movements was a gradual revolutionary process which opened up the route for anarchists and socialists on the left, coupled with reactions by the conservative establishment against the progressives. Generally, the state had a weak but oppressive role, operating by a network of threats and physical force. The social fabric was itself weak and in this context the seeds of the civil war and Franco's rise to power were sown.

*Constitutional crisis*   The years between 1917 and 1936 epitomize a period of crisis which witnessed the fall of the monarchy in 1931 and the republican constitution which displayed profound political and social divisions. Religious persecution, class struggles, separatism and the law of the defence of the public brought about the end of liberalism. The army, which was always an important political institution, during this period discarded its grading structure based on a privilege of birth and became more politicized. It seemed that all the tensions growing out of the nineteenth and early twentieth centuries were brought together in the 1931 constitution and finally erupted into the civil war of 1936–9.

Before outlining the events of the later twentieth century and the background to the 1978 constitution, a brief description of the successive constitutions of the nineteenth and early twentieth centuries which reflect the different characteristics of that period will be provided.

## The Political Swings in the Constitutions during the Nineteenth and Twentieth Centuries

The constitutions which were created successively during the nineteenth and twentieth centuries reflect the political and social conditions of each period. They highlight the tension between the moderates and the radicals and between those who favoured national sovereignty and those who favoured sovereignty of the monarchy. This section describes briefly the content and characteristics of the significant constitutions of the period.

*1808: El Estatuto (or La Carta) of Bayona*   This was created personally by Napoleon and its existence was really only theoretical since it was not a national law, and had no authoritative or legally binding status. It was more of a charter than a constitution. The *Estatuto* contained two distinctive parts: first, a separation of powers and a fragmented power of legislation and, second, a genuine programme of reform which included codification, lower interior taxes, reduction of inherited privileges and separation of public wealth from the Crown. The *Estatuto* also contained a general declaration of rights and this highlighted reforms such as suppression of privileges, protection of property, right to freedom of movement and abolition of torture. Although the *Estatuto* had no legally binding force, it demonstrated an intention for political and social reform that would signify a reduction of the power bases of the nobility and empowerment of the bourgeoisie.

*1812: constitution of Cádiz*   This was the first genuine constitution after the invasion of Napoleon and it demonstrated a rejection of Napoleon's invasion. Napoleon failed to gain public support and this constitution arose out of the war of independence. Nevertheless, many of the French ideas of liberalism and national sovereignty were adopted. This constitution was a constitution of the people, containing a number of important principles including division of powers between the legislature, the executive and the judiciary; the deputies in the *Cortes* of Cádiz to represent the state in its entirety rather than each deputy representing sectional or territorial elements; and the principle of rationalism in order to establish some order for the state's administrative, judicial, territorial, and fiscal and budgetary aspects. Laws would have to be reformed by following prescribed procedures. This constitution did not contain a table or list of rights or liberties.

*1834: the Estatuto Real*   This *Estatuto* highlighted a reaction by the moderates against the progressives. It therefore provided a declaration of absolute monarchy as well as a declaration of nullity of the constitution and decrees created by the Cádiz parliament. This was a constitution given by the monarchy by virtue of its sovereign power and the *Estatuto* provided that the monarch was to share power with the *Cortes* but without those powers being formally separated. It was a brief constitutional document with only 50 articles since it was limited to regulating the organization of the *Cortes*, their structure, composition and functions. It was also a flexible constitution which did not contain any strict procedure for bringing about legal reform. Nor did it contain a declaration of rights. The *Estatuto* was characterized by a principle of moderation, seeking a balance between order and liberty and between tradition and new ideas.

*The 1837 constitution*   This was the first constitution of the reign of Isabel II. The main feature of this period was its political swings between progressive and moderate agendas. This constant antagonism between the two political forces owed its existence to a number of factors, including freedom of the press, powers of the monarchy, structure and powers of the *Cortes*, and municipal autonomy. The role of the Crown as a moderating force was open to question since the Crown preserved powers of appointment and dismissal of ministers as well as the power to dissolve the *Cortes*. A problem which manifested itself during this period was that Queen Isabel allied herself with the moderates rather than remain neutral. During the period there was also evidence of political corruption. The first constitution of this era was generally liberal and progressive and contained various promises. It also contained a declaration of rights which highlighted the influence of philosophies of positivism and utilitarianism. Finally, although the constitution contained a preamble which provided for national sovereignty, the substantive parts of the constitution did not reinforce the preamble. Thus the 1837 constitution might be regarded as a statement of progressive principles which were not developed in substance.

*The 1845 constitution*   This constitution returned to moderate principles and thus substituted national sovereignty for sovereignty to be shared by the Crown and *Cortes*. In effect the constitution increased the powers of Queen Isabel II and correspondingly reduced the autonomy of the *Cortes*. It established a higher parliamentary chamber to be appointed by the queen from among the nobility, the army and the church administration. The congress, the lower parliamentary chamber, was also altered by conservative reforms. For example, election of the congress was reduced to a franchise of 1 per cent of the population. The new declaration of rights also abolished the trial by jury system and other rights became subject to later legal restrictions. The constitution was influenced by catholicism.

*The 1869 constitution*   This constitution was a result of the 1868 revolution which occurred as a reaction to the country's financial crisis as well as to contradictions within the moderate regime which led to problems in the parliamentary system, increasing loss of support of the Crown, and a rupture between the Crown and public. None of the governments was able to provide order or stability. Following the revolution, this constitution meant, above all, the affirmation of radical liberalism as against the doctrinaire model of liberalism which had dominated previous constitutional texts. This was the first democratic constitution with the *Cortes* to be elected by universal male suffrage, and these voters would decree and sanction the constitution. This constitution affirmed national sovereignty and the principle of division of powers. It was also revolutionary and progressive in character, although with a relatively simple reform procedure. It contained the most extensive of all previous declarations of rights, providing a long, but not exhaustive, list which would include freedom of religious beliefs, recognition of universal suffrage and recognition of collective rights such as freedom of association.

*The 1876 constitution*   This constitution was created after the monarchy had been restored. Alfonso XII became king of Spain in December 1874. He brought with him a restoration of the moderate form of liberalism. This constitution of 30 June 1876 tried to avoid each political party establishing its own constitution and sought to recognize all existing political views. It was, therefore, a pluralistic constitution, sometimes described by Spanish commentators as 'eclectic' and was also flexible in its approach. The aim was to establish itself in a political position equidistant from the moderate text of 1845 and the radical text of 1869. This endowed the constitution with an artificial character which would be difficult to sustain. The constitution was based on an agreement between Crown and *Cortes*, giving joint sovereignty to the king and *Cortes*, but it did not make clear how their powers would be shared. It was also a flexible constitution which could be modified relatively easily.

*The 1931 constitution* This constitution was created after the regime of Primo de Rivera had ended. By 1929, his dictatorship had lost its impulse and initial support. Alfonso XII had to abdicate after the municipal elections of 1931 which marked a vote of censure for the monarchy. A revolutionary committee took its place and brought in a new constitution in June of 1931. A number of serious issues had to be dealt with, such as religion, since the church had traditionally been connected to the establishment. The 1931 constitution declared that the state would have no official religion, would have a secular education and would recognize divorce. The regional question was also important: the constitution had to find a solution to the problem of bringing unity while preserving recognition of the various regions and their special characteristics and needs. The solution offered was that of an integral state which recognized the autonomy of regions and municipalities, but in which, for example, Castilian was declared the official language. This limited autonomy was later regarded as having sown seeds of discontent among the regions. The state was also suffering severe economic problems which demanded protection for the more vulnerable classes. Women were allowed to vote for the first time and, according to Merino-Blanco (1996), the electoral register was modified to prevent manipulation of the electorate.

This constitution did nothing to eradicate the growing divisions in Spanish society which had been building up since the early part of the nineteenth century. In the opinion of Heywood (1995), these divisions 'hardened into a series of bitter confrontations which pitched republicans against monarchists, anti-clericals against the Catholic Church, regionalists against centralists and workers against employers'. This situation, according to Heywood at least, made inevitable the civil war that gripped and devastated Spain between 1936 and 1939. The civil war frustrated attempts at regeneration and, as noted by Casanova (1987), brought a period of rupture from the previous regime.

*The Dictatorship of Franco and the Subsequent Establishment of Democracy*

The civil war began in July 1936 and lasted until March 1939. The nationalists defeated the republicans and gave rise to a regime that itself developed a new constitution through a series of seven fundamental laws. This culminated, on Franco's death, in the establishment of a constitutional monarchy.

According to Heywood (1995), Franco's regime showed no intention of promoting national reconciliation. Rather, it was a rhetorical regime with emphasis on distinction between the victors and the defeated and it confirmed the deep divisions that had existed in Spanish history. Generally, it was very bureaucratic and centralist, with Franco holding the vision of a Spain which was *una, grande y libre*: united, large and free. The regime did become less repressive during the 1950s, and during the 1960s economic growth and modernization strengthened some of the support for Franco. However, he faced renewed opposition towards the end of the 1960s and he responded to that opposition with a return to repression, demonstrated dramatically by the executions in 1975 of five men who were accused of killing policemen and civil guards. Franco died on 20 November 1975 and after that date Spain was free to initiate a transition to democracy.

From a constitutional point of view, Franco's regime provided an important foundation for the eventual settlement in 1978. Franco's dictatorship was a sovereign dictatorship and as the official 'chief of state' Franco was empowered to constitute a new state. Over a period of some 30 years, he introduced a fragmented series of laws called '*Leyes Fundamentales*' on employment, creation of the *Cortes*, Spanish citizenship, referendum, succession to the chief of state, fundamental principles of the national movement and a so-called 'organic law of the state'. Through these laws were formalized a number of dogmatic principles such as legislation being inspired by the doctrine of the Catholic Church, and a traditional, Catholic and representative monarchy to provide the political framework of the state.

There were a number of stages by which Franco's regime developed. During the period 1936–7 there was a monarchic restoration, though this monarchy would rest on the personality of the *Caudillo de Espana y de la Cruzada* and on the *Generalisimo de los Ejercitos*. Thus the chief of state was a personal office. Franco had the support of the army, of the traditional and conservative classes and of the church. This church backing continued during the early 1940s. That support, together with the shadow of the Second World War, enabled Franco to gain democratic support for his regime, reducing his image as an absolutist autocrat. In the late 1940s, his position was reinforced by his anti-communist stance and by signs of economic reconstruction.

An issue of considerable concern during the 1950s would be that of who and what should succeed this personal dictatorship. During this time, also, Spain gained economic strength through foreign investments, business negotiations and a tourism boom which allowed industrial development and a capitalist expansion. This period was also relatively liberal, allowing the press and associations to gain some influence. During 1967–75, an Organic Law of the State introduced a monarchy for the succession of General Franco and during this period there was a transition from an absolute to a limited monarchy. With the death of Franco in 1975, the Organic Law of the

State of 1967 entered into force, as did the Law of Succession of 1969, by which General Franco had elected Don Juan Carlos of Bourbon to be his successor. The new king, Juan Carlos I, lacked sovereign power since, as a result of Franco's laws, he did not inherit Franco's prerogatives. Therefore, he could not monopolize effective decision-making power. Thus, as a consequence of Franco's laws, there was an automatic transition from an absolutist monarchy to a limited constitutional monarchy.

A referendum on the Law for Political Reform took place on 15 December 1976. This took Spain into a new era. The authoritarian system had paved the way for a democratic system and a new constitution. In 1977, the new Law for Political Reform effectively dismantled the previous Fundamental Laws and conferred on the monarchy a legitimacy derived by popular consensus. In 1977, there were general elections and a constitutional reform. The king sought the easiest and least conflictual route for transforming his authoritative monarchy into a democracy. The *Cortes* were democratized and a democratic constitution was created which came into force in 1978. It is that constitution which provides a basis and framework for Spain's existing legal system.

## Today's Spanish Legal System

The rest of this book will provide a description of the major aspects of the Spanish law and legal system which it is hoped will provide a basis from which students may build their knowledge of the substantive parts of that law and legal system. Before taking the reader to the more detailed description, the remainder of this chapter will provide a few background observations.

Spanish law is classified into public law and private law rules. The distinctions arise from the nature of the objective or interest protected. Thus public law generally protects the interests of the state and its institutions and organisms as a societal interest, while private law is usually concerned with the private interest of the person and, indirectly through that person, the interests of society. Private law tends to have a proprietorial character, in contrast with the public law focus on general interests. Those classes of law which fall into the sphere of private law are civil law and mercantile law, while those areas covered by public law principles are constitutional law, administrative law, tax law, labour law and social security, procedural law, and criminal law.

Spanish law is also a codified system of law derived from natural law philosophies and influenced particularly by the French Civil Code of 1804. Spanish law contains three codes: the Civil Code which deals inter alia with the system of hierarchy of laws, a Criminal Code and a Commercial Code. These codes have been renewed and revised periodically and are supplemented by other laws which have their own place in the normative hierarchy. Spain also has a background of local law influences which still shape today's Spanish law as well as the provisions created by the autonomous communities.

The influence of European Community law is as evident in Spanish law as it is in the law of any other member state. This will merit a discussion of Spain's entry into the European Community and an outline of the way European Community law has been accommodated by the Spanish legal system.

## The Spanish Legal Professions

The Spanish legal system has many characteristics different from the legal systems of the common law world. This itself makes for a distinct legal professional structure and it is therefore appropriate to provide a brief description of the practical legal environment in Spain. This information is provided in greater detail in Merino-Blanco (1996) and I have relied heavily on that source.

On completion of a Spanish law degree one becomes *licenciado en derecho* and is qualified to practise law. The Spanish law degree has a number of compulsory law subjects as well as some compulsory subjects relevant to each specific university and some optional subjects. Normally, the degree takes approximately five years to complete and covers a broad range of subjects. After completing the degree, the graduate has a number of options for pursuing a legal career. The different possible roles in law include abogado, procurador, notary, civil servant, fiscal, judge, public registrar, judicial secretary and law academic. Each of these roles has its own programme of entrance.

### Abogado

The *abogado* is a practising lawyer who provides advice and conciliation and defends both public and private interests. In order to become an *abogado* the individual who is *licenciado en derecho* must be a member of a *Colegio de Abogados* which are located in all Spain's provincial capitals and other major cities. Although there is no official training period for *abogados*, graduates will frequently follow a special course of legal practice or will join a law firm as a *pasante*, which is similar to a trainee solicitor in the UK. *Abogados* are obliged to give free advice to those entitled to legal aid and will be compensated by the state. Contingency fees are prohibited, as are higher fees dependent on winning the case. There are many *abogados* in Spain (approximately 98 000) and competition is fierce. This leads many law graduates to opt for other careers either within law or in business and commerce.

Procurador

A *procurador* is a lawyer who acts under a power of attorney on behalf of the person who requires his or her services. The *procurador* acts on that person's behalf in the courts and other official departments and often he or she is hired by the *abogado*. Similar to *abogados*, a *procurador* must be a member of a *Colegio de Procuradores*.

*Notary*

Where parties enter into a legal transaction, the notary provides authenticity for the documents created as part of the transaction. The notary may draft the documentation or provide advice on the drafting, explaining the legal consequences of the provisions contained in the documents. The notary has a neutral role in that he or she does not act on behalf of one of the parties. Documents which have been authenticated by a notary are presumed to be representative of the truth and accuracy of the circumstances, unless falsity is proved in criminal proceedings. The objective is to provide legal certainty to the parties and thereby to prevent conflicts between them over the trans-action concerned. It is necessary to obtain authentification of a document by the notary in transactions involving real estate, company constitutional docu-ments, donations between spouses, contracts which determine or alter the economic consequences of marriage, mortgages, creation of easements and declaration of heirs. In order to become a notary, the law graduate must pass a very competitive examination and must become a member of a *Colegio de Notarios*.

*Civil Servant*

A large number of civil servants are law graduates and they enter the civil service by taking a competitive examination. Some become diplomats while other branches of the civil service, more directly related to law, include the Ministry of Justice, which supports the judiciary and the public prosecutors, for example, by organizing the administration and running of the courts.

*Fiscal*

The *Ministerio Fiscal* is also a constitutional body which gives to fiscals the role of upholding the law and promoting the application of justice in the defence of the rights of citizens and the public interest, as well as the independence of the courts. Fiscals carry out these duties by being involved in the criminal law process as public prosecutors, in addition to being involved in proceedings which concern guardianship as well as cases concerning the civil status of natural persons.

*Judge*

All judges, apart from justices of the peace, hold a law degree and have either passed a competitive examination or followed a course with final examination or have been selected from among lawyers with at least six years' experience. Magistrates have a higher status than judges in Spain and these are appointed by being highest in the hierarchy of judges, or by already being a judge and passing a competitive examination, or by being selected from among lawyers of at least 10 years' experience. Magistrates of the Supreme Court must have at least 10 years' experience as a magistrate and 20 years as a member of the judiciary and one of the five magistrates in each chamber of the Supreme Court will be chosen from among lawyers with at least 20 years' experience in the area of law of the chamber to which he or she is appointed.

*Public Registrar*

The public registrar has the role of entering documents onto an official register for public access to the information contained in those documents. For example, the registrar will check company constitutional documents and then enter them onto the commerical register, as is required by the Commercial Code and the company laws.

*Judicial Secretary*

These hold a law degree and their role is to assist the judiciary in the administration of the courts. For example, they hold the court documents and depositions as well as keeping the books and records of the court's judicial activities.

*Law Academic*

In order to become a law academic it is necessary to study for a doctorate. The doctoral course involves following a number of courses and submitting a long research essay before proceeding with the doctoral thesis. After completing the thesis, it is possible to become a *profesor titular* by defending one's research before a tribunal and later, in a similar but more rigorous fashion, to seek a position as *Catedrático de Derecho*. These positions are very competitive and the tribunal is a public and very formal process.

## Sources of Reference in Spanish Legal Study

The student of Spanish law will find the following publishers particularly useful: The Boletín Oficial del Estado in which major legal reforms and reform projects are published. Major publishers of Spanish laws and texts include, Aranzadi, Civitas, Tecnos, Tirant lo Blanch and Marcial Pons. Aranzadi publishes the laws and court judgments. Case law itself has an interpretative role and judgments therefore tend to be much shorter than most English law reports.

## References and Further Reading

*General Texts*

Calvo Meijide, Alberto, *Introducción al Derecho Público y Privado* (1994, Prensa y Ediciones Iberoamericanos, Madrid).
Ellingham, Mark and Fisher, John, *Spain: The Rough Guide*, 5th edn (1991, Rough Guides, London).
Heywood, Paul, *The Government and Politics of Spain* (1995, Macmillan, London).
Merino-Blanco, Elena, *The Spanish Legal System* (1996, Sweet & Maxwell, London).
Olivan López, Fernando, Ezquierra Serrano, Maria del Rosario and Muñoz Blasquez, Fernando Manuel, *Introducción al Derecho*, 3rd edn (1993, Tecnos, Madrid).

*On the Constitutional History*

Cazorla Prieto, Luís María and Arnaldo Alcubilla, Enrique, *Temas de Derecho Constitucional y Derecho Administrativo* (1988, Marcial Pons, Madrid).
González Casanova, J.A., *Teoria del Estado y Derecho Constitucional*, 3rd edn (1987, Vicens Universidad, Barcelona).
Martínez Cuadrado, Miguel, 'La Constitución Española de 1978 en la Historia del

Constitucionalismo Español', in Alberto Predieri and Eduardo García de Enterría, *La Constitucion de 1978* (1981, Civitas, Madrid).

Perez Royo, Javier, 'La Reforma de La Constitución' (1986) 22 *Revista de Derecho Político*, 7–60.

Preston, Paul, *The Triumph of Democracy in Spain* (1986, Routledge, London).

Sánchez, Agesta Luís, *Curso de Derecho Constitucional Comparado* (1980) Universidad de Madrid, Madrid.

# 2 The Spanish Constitution of 1978

The Spanish Constitution of 1978 symbolizes the end of the Franco regime and the optimism of a new democracy. As Heywood (1995) remarks, the constitution 'situates the country firmly within the tradition of pluralist, liberal democracies'. In creating the constitution, the aim was to establish a political system within the Western tradition which would guarantee to citizens certain freedoms and would offer to all political groups access to the political process as well as offering to the regions a degree of political autonomy. The 1978 constitution itself combines a progressive approach, offering extensive individual rights, with a strong role for the state, in the hope that the constitution would not suffer the same fate as those of the nineteenth century.

The 1978 constitution was the result of a multi-party pact. By contrast, all the previous constitutions, apart from that of 1876, had been the product of one political movement. This time the aim was for a consensus upon which all parties would be agreed. This approach could have led to a merely procedural document providing only rules on process, yet the 1978 constitution itself contains extensive substantive rules, particularly in Titles I and II.

A number of influences can be identified, especially the models provided by the Italian and West German constitutions. For example, from the 1947 Italian Constitution the Spanish document appears to have borrowed ideas for the *Poder Judicial* – the organization of the judiciary; the *estado regional*, a unified state but one which recognizes a degree of independence for the regions; the promotion of public powers; and a constitution created by popular initiative. From the German Fundamental Law of Bonn of 1949 the Spaniards appear to have been inspired by the concept of the social state and the democratic rule of law. Other identifiable influences include the rights and liberties available in the Portuguese Constitution of 1976, the ombudsman present in the Nordic states, as well as the arbitral role of the king, and the regulation of the motion of censure which may be found in the French Constitution of 1958.

## Creation of the 1978 Constitution

A little over a year after the death of Franco and the accession to the throne of King Juan Carlos I on 22 November 1975, the *Cortes Generales* (the Spanish parliamentary chambers) introduced a Law of Political Reform which was approved by referendum on 15 December 1976. Although this law did not derogate or modify the previous *Leyes Fundamentales* of the former regime, it altered the basis of the complex structure on which those laws were founded by proclaiming the principle of popular sovereignty and creating a bicameralist parliament which would have two chambers: the *Congreso de los Diputados* (congress of deputies) and the *Senado* (senate) both of which would be elected by universal suffrage. Article 3 of the Law of Political Reform made provision for the possibility of constitutional reform which would require an absolute majority of both chambers and the approval of the proposed reform by referendum. The Law of Political Reform was itself approved by 76.6 per cent of the electorate, of which 94 per cent voted. In short, it was an instrumental law for the transition towards a formally democratic regime and towards a monarchy compatible with that regime.

As noted, as a consequence of the Law of Political Reform, the parliament came to have two chambers, the congress of deputies and the senate, both elected by universal suffrage and proportional representation. The congress of deputies was given the power to initiate constitutional reform; the senate would vet the constitutional reform of the congress. Finally, since sovereignty would rest with the people, the king would sanction the reform of the fundamental laws with public support established by referendum. All the political groups gave support to the monarchy and the king renounced all future constitutional power, leaving to the government and the parliament the decision for proceeding with constitutional reform.

The political context in which the constitution was to be created was much more liberal than it had been before Franco's death. This would influence the character of the constitution. For example, there had been an extension of political freedoms by which the government provided for the right of political association and, in February 1977, permitted by decree the legalization of political parties and the freedom of expression. There was also a revision of the legislation on terrorism and a decriminalization of the exercise of political and union freedoms. These developments gave rise to an extension of regionalist and nationalist movements throughout Spain, as well as a growth of different political groups. The Communist Party was also legalized and a coalition called the *Unión de Centro Democrático* was established. Spain was also keen to establish an international role and in July 1977 applied for full membership of the EEC. This would further indicate to the outside world Spain's willingness to move towards a democratic system.

On 15 June 1977, general elections were held for the congress of deputies and for the senate. In this election the large and moderate parties were favoured. In the congress of deputies the breakdown of votes and seats was as follows: *Unión de Centro Democrático* (UCD) 34.7 per cent votes and 165 seats, *Partido Socialista Obrero Español* (PSOE) 29.2 per cent of the votes and 118 seats, *Partido Comunista de España* (PCE) 9.2 per cent and 20 seats, *Alianza Popular* (AP) 8.2 per cent and 16 seats, *Pacte Democratic per Catalunya* (PDC) 2.7 per cent and 11 seats, *Partido Nacionalista Vasco* (PNV) (the Basque Nationalist Party) 1.6 per cent and eight seats. In the senate the UCD occupied 106 of the 207 seats, thus having an absolute majority. The PSOE had only 47 seats.

The party system had effectively been rationalized during the 1977 elections. As Preston (1986) observes,

> the pre-electoral confusion of over 300 political parties had been reduced on 15 June to a four-party system and the voters had opted overwhelmingly for moderation. In opinion polls, four out of every five Spaniards described themselves as belonging to the area between right and left of centre.

As soon as it met on 13 July 1977, the congress of deputies agreed on the creation of a Constitutional Commission. This commission would have the role of preparing a Constitutional Plan to be processed according to the provisions of the Law of Political Reform and the rules of both parliamentary chambers. The *Comisión de Asuntos Constitucionales y Libertades Públicas* was created in accordance with the regulation of the congress of deputies on 22 October 1977. This commission established a *Ponencia* (round table) consisting of seven members representing all the parliamentary political groups: 3 from the UCD; 1 from the PSOE; 1 from the PCE; 1 from the *Movimiento Comunista* (a Trotskyist movement independent of the PCE); and 1 from the AP. The composition of the *Ponencia* may be criticized on at least two grounds: the imbalance in representation between the centre party and the socialists, and the notable absence of representation of the *Minoría Vasco*.

The Constitutional Commission worked on drafts created by each member of the *Ponencia*. Its meetings were not held in public, thus making it difficult to establish either the initial positions of each group or the nature of their respective drafts. However, it is clear that Spanish politics were guided by a consensus approach during that period. Consensus marks a position in which not just the decision of the majority prevails, but only what will be acceptable to all groups who are to coexist. In other words, it is something to which each party must defer above its own specific values or ideals. Of course this can make the decision-making procedure more complex, since groups have to distinguish between positions which they find unacceptable and those with which they are prepared to compromise. Sometimes this leads to empty agreements or compromises which are simply a postponement of later confrontations. For the negotiations in 1977–8, the support of certain parties was necessary while others could not be accommodated without losing the basic objectives of constitutionalism; for example, the support of the Socialist Party was required but to offer to the Basques complete independence would not correspond with the aims of the constitutional settlement. The *Ponencia* published a draft constitution on 5 January 1978 on which the deputies and the parliamentary groups could formulate their amendments.

Once the amendments were submitted, the *Ponencia* met again to prepare a definitive draft which could now be deliberated upon publicly in the Constitutional Commission. The new draft was published on 17 April 1978. The Constitutional Commission initiated the debate on this draft on 5 May. During the first few days of this debate the consensus approach seemed to be abandoned, with some majority decisions being taken which were sustained only by the votes of the UCD and the AP. However, the fierce reaction to this by the other parties forced a return to the consensus approach. The differences were settled privately and were later validated by public debate, and the process continued. The Constitutional Commission finished its involvement on 20 June and the debate continued afterwards in the *Pleno* – the full house of the congress of deputies – during 4–21 July. The first additional provision which gives express recognition to the historical laws of the *foral* territories (regions, such as the old kingdom of Navarra, which historically had a degree of independence) appeared as a result of these negotiations in which the Basque group wanted the recognition of the right to autonomy.

Apart from this obstacle, the draft constitution passed to the senate, where there were a further 1128 amendments, which ultimately did not result in any significant changes, to the text. After a debate in the Commission (18 August) and then in the *Pleno* (25 September to 5 October) where opposition was repeated to the additional provision for historic rights of local territories the text was approved by the senate and then passed to a mixed commission of senators and deputies, provided for in the Law on Political Reform of 1977. The deliberations of this mixed commission also took place in private during 16–25 October. On 31 October the resulting definitive text was approved by the parliament separately and simultaneously by the congress of deputies and the senate, with a very reduced number of negative votes and an abstention by the Basque representatives. The campaign for achieving public approval of the text was begun on 20 November 1978. In the subsequent referendum which took place on 6 December 1978 the constitution was approved by 87.78 per cent of the voters (58.97 per cent of the electorate). There were 7.38 per cent of the votes (5.25 per cent of the electorate) against the official draft and the remaining votes were blank or null votes. In all, 32.89 per cent of the electorate abstained, most of these being from the Basque region. The constitution was sanctioned by the king on 27 December and was published and entered into force on 29 December 1978.

For Spain, 29 December 1978 is an important date in recent political history. The constitution would provide a new framework for political and legal developments and would mark the arrival of democracy. However, a number of flaws in the constitutional settlement achieved would lead to a number of subsequent political and legal problems. For example, the constitution did not receive the approval of the whole population: some 33 per cent of eligible voters did not vote and in the Basque region only 49 per cent voted. The Basque region's views were not represented in the *Ponencia*, which would become a problem for Spain in her search for a balance between the unified nation state and the demands of the different regions. In some ways this highlights the ambiguity left by the constitution. For example, the term 'state' has many possible meanings. The final text of the constitution also left unclear the position and role of the monarchy.

Before considering the structure and contents of the constitutional text, a brief outline of the procedures necessary for reforming the constitution will be provided.

## Reform of the Constitution

The 1978 constitution does not prohibit reform of its contents or text. Thus since its creation some political groups have continued to air their opposition to certain aspects of the constitution, but no party has presented any proposal for reform. However, according to Rubio Llorente (1993), this lack of any reform proposal probably owes more to the procedural difficulty of effecting a reform than to the fact that the constitution is based on a solid consensus. Indeed, the complexity of the procedures leads commentators to label the 1978 constitution as a 'rigid' constitution.

Chapter X of the constitution regulates the process of constitutional reform establishing two distinct procedures with different levels of complexity depending on the extent of the proposed reform. The more complex procedure, laid out in Article 168, would have to be followed where the proposed reform would lead to the creation of a whole new constitution or one that purported to affect certain titles in the existing text, such as proposed changes to fundamental rights and public freedoms or aspects relating to the Crown. The reason for the more complex procedure in these circumstances is that these fields are considered to require stability. Consequently, if a reform of another part of the constitution would affect these parts, that reform would also necessitate use of the more complex procedure. In order to retain their stability, reform of these procedures does not depend solely on the decision of the *Cortes*, but requires the involvement of the electorate. Other reform proposals would follow a less complicated procedure, which is the same procedure as that required for creating new legislation through the presentation of a proposal or plan.

For the simple procedure, the initiative for constitutional reform may be exercised by the government, by the congress of deputies or by the senate, or by the assemblies of the autonomous communities. It is not possible for a reform to be instigated by a popular initiative. If the proposal is initiated by the congress of deputies, the rules of the congress require that the proposal must have the support of two parliamentary groups or of 25 deputies. A proposal put forward by the senate requires 50 senators who need not necessarily belong to the same political group. The two chambers may reject a reform proposal. Under the procedure which is similar to that for creating legislation, reform proposals need a favourable vote by three-fifths of the members of each chamber, a higher majority than that required for any legislative procedure. If there should be no agreement between the two chambers this would be attempted by a commission party of deputies and senators who would present a text to be voted on by the congress and the senate. If there was no approval or agreement but there was an absolute majority of the senate, the congress could approve the reform by a two-thirds majority. The reform, approved by the *Cortes Generales*, would be submitted to a referendum if that was requested within 15 days of the approval of the reform by a tenth of the members of whichever chamber. Once approved, the reform would need to be sanctioned and promulgated by the king in order for it formally to become law.

The more complex special procedure is initiated by the two chambers which would have to state the principle on which to proceed with the reform and it would have to be approved by a two-thirds majority in each chamber. If the reform should be approved in both chambers it would then proceed to the dissolution of the *Cortes* and the calling of new elections. The newly elected chambers would then have to ratify the decision of the preceding chambers. It is suggested by De Otto (1993) that this decision would need to have a two-thirds majority, although he notes that the rules of the senate appear only to demand a simple majority. The reform proposal will require the approval of a two-thirds majority of each chamber. Then the reform will be submitted to a referendum for its ratification, effectively requiring a second involvement by the electorate, which may be difficult in practice.

This constitutional rigidity seeks to balance stability with the possibility of change, but the constitution is criticized, in particular, for its complex procedure which, in reality, means that the provisions protected by it are almost impossible to change. Some commentators also suggest that the complex procedure extends too broadly. The constitutional rigidity attempts to guarantee the continuity of constitutional principles and provisions and limits the competence of the ordinary legislative organs. In a sense, according to Cazorla Prieto and Arnaldo Alcubilla (1988), the rigidity is a form of defence that assures the supremacy of the constitution and preserves its stable character. At the same time the constitution, in order to survive, must be able to adapt to social and historical changes.

In reality, the second procedure is so complex and costly that these aspects of the constitution would appear to be virtually immune from attempts at reform. Furthermore, the fact that the legislative assemblies of the autonomous communities can instigate reform has been criticized because these are not strictly constitutional organs. However, this possibility does illustrate a definite role for the autonomous communities in constitutional affairs. Another criticism which might be made is that of the requirement of qualified majorities. De Otto (1993) suggests that this creates an imbalance in weight of those voting for and against change. Those who do not want change effectively have weightier votes. On the other hand, it could be argued that the need for a higher majority assures the legitimacy of the reform when that higher majority is achieved. In summary, the aspects of the constitution which are protected by the complex procedure are those aspects which define the basic principles of the constitutional democracy. The rights and liberties of the people are so fundamentally essential that it ought to be difficult to alter them. On the other hand, they may need some alteration in order to reinforce them and not necessarily to take them away. Thus it ought, at least in theory, to be possible to alter even these aspects of the constitution, but the seriousness of such alteration has to be reflected by the procedure adopted. Needless to say, to date there have been no such reforms of the constitution since its entry into force!

## Structure of the Constitution

The constitution has 169 articles and, apart from the 1812 constitution, is the most extensive in Spanish constitutional history since the beginning of the nineteenth century. The text contains a preamble, a preliminary title, ten separate and substantive titles, four additional provisions, nine transitional provisions, a derogation of previous laws which oppose or contradict the constitution, and a final provision.

The preamble sets out the principles which form the framework of the constitution. From this point of view it is appropriate to provide a translation of the preamble:

> The Spanish nation, wishing to establish justice, liberty and security and to promote the well being of the State's citizens, in the use of their sovereignty, proclaims its intention:
> To guarantee democratic life within a Constitution which conforms to a just social and economic order;
> To consolidate a rule of law which assures that the law will act as an expression of the people's intentions;
> To protect all Spaniards and residents in Spain in the exercise of their human rights, their cultures, traditions, languages and institutions;
> To promote cultural and economic advance in order to assure for everyone a dignified quality of life;
> To establish a democratic and advanced society; and
> To collaborate in the strengthening of peaceful relations and cooperation between the populations of the world.

The principles and values set out in the preamble are regarded by Casanova (1987) as the great political decisions which express the intentions of the Spanish people. They are expressed in the style of the purest liberal and democratic tradition, and are strengthened by the three contemporary demands of a social and economic system equipped to treat all citizens justly and to enable them to develop to their full potential; a legal system which guarantees and protects the fundamental rights of people living in Spain; and a universal international policy based on peace and solidarity. These principles and values are later developed in the substantive text of the constitution.

The preliminary title, which Casanova classifies as the section of the constitution which contains the great constitutional definitions, details the principles set out in the preamble. In this way the preliminary title provides an ideological political formula organized into a legal and social structure. Thus the section contains principles such as national sovereignty, and the guaranteed right of autonomy for nationalities and regions. The section also provides definitions for parliamentary sovereignty, political parties, unions, employers' organizations and the function of the armed forces.

Article 1 defines the social and democratic state as one which fosters, as the superior values of its legal order, freedom, justice, equality and political pluralism. Article 1 also provides that national sovereignty resides in the people and that the political form of the state is that of a parliamentary monarchy. Under Article 2, the constitution recognizes and guarantees the right to autonomy of the nationalities and regions that make up the Spanish nation, combined with national solidarity, and the constitution also recognizes the different cultures of these regions. Article 6 provides that the political parties reflect political pluralism in accordance with the formation and manifestation of the wishes of the people and such parties are regarded as a fundamental instrument of political participation. Article 3 provides that Castilian is the official language of the state, while recognizing and respecting the status of the other languages in the autonomous communities. Article 4 provides a description of the national flag, providing that this shall be displayed in autonomous communities next to their own flag on official buildings and offices, and Article 5 declares that Madrid is the Spanish capital. The section ends with Article 9, stating that both citizens and public authorities will be bound by the constitution and the legal system. Article 9 lays out the principle of the rule of law, which is that the constitution guarantees the principle of legality, a hierarchy of legal rules, publicity of legal rules, non-retroactive penalties or restrictions on individual rights, legal security and responsibility and prevention of arbitrary behaviour by public bodies. Under Article 9, equality appears not only to be a political concept but one which is also economic and social, and the state is understood to be an equal society.

The first title of the constitution is subdivided into five chapters. The first chapter provides for the protection of Spanish nationality, sets the age of majority at 18 years, and clarifies the rights for which both Spanish nationals and foreign residents will be treated alike. Arguably, the most important of these is the second chapter which is divided into two sections, each concerned with rights and liberties. The first section covers those fundamental rights and public freedoms which, in chapter four, are granted the highest form of protection under the constitution, and the second section sets out the rights and duties of citizens. The third chapter provides the guiding principles of social and economic policy; and the fifth chapter sets out when citizens' rights and liberties will be suspended.

What is clear from the first title is that the rights provided by the constitution are not all identical; nor do they enjoy equal effectiveness or protection. Commentators make three distinctions: fundamental rights in a strict sense, constitutional rights and guiding principles of social and economic policy. The strict sense fundamental rights are found in Article 14, which sets out the principle of equality, and then in Articles 15–29. These include the right to physical and moral integrity; the freedom of ideology, religion and beliefs; freedom and personal security and *habeas corpus*; protection of reputation, and personal and family privacy; protection of domicile; confidentiality in communications without their being intruded upon; right to choose residence freely and to move freely within the national territory, and to enter and leave Spain freely; freedom of expression and academic freedom; right to receive correct information; right of assembly and to demonstrate; right of association; right of universal suffrage and of access to public office; right to obtain effective judicial protection and to procedural rights; right to education and instruction; right to unionize freely and to strike; and right of individual and collective petition. It is clear from this list that the fundamental rights and liberties include individual, political and social rights.

These rights are classified in the constitution as fundamental rights because they are protected by the highest of guarantees. They also have direct legal and binding effect. Article 53.1 provides that all public bodies are bound by these rights. The rights have immediate effect and do not require further legislation for their implementation. They are not mere principles for policy direction. Their essential contents are guaranteed. Only by law can the exercise of these rights be regulated and that law must not contradict the basic contents of these rights. Citizens can protect this category of rights in the ordinary courts by a preferential and summary procedure, established by a 1978 Law on Judicial Protection of the Fundamental Rights of the Person. A citizen may have direct access to the constitutional court to clarify the rights by way of a special procedure called 'recurso de amparo'. Any of the rights and liberties within this category may also be protected from the actions of third parties.

The second category of rights comprises the constitutional rights outlined in Articles 30–38 under the heading of rights and duties of citizens. Technically, these are not fundamental rights but are merely constitutional rights. However, this category includes some very important rights such as the right to private property and to succession; the right to work; the right to collective bargaining and to adopt means of collective conflict; and freedom of enterprise within the framework of the market economy. Generally, this category of rights enjoys similar status to the fundamental rights but they do not enjoy the preferential and summary judicial protection that the rights in the first chapter of this title enjoy.

The third chapter in the first title sets out the 'guiding principles of social and economic policy'. These lack the qualities of the rights set out in the second chapter, since they are not directly legally binding. They do not impose an objective limit on the legislator with an essential content and their effectiveness depends on the actions of the legislator. Effectively, they require further legislation in order to have any practical effect. Then their effectiveness depends on the extent to which the legislation follows their direction. They tend to be rhetorical in nature and cover a wide range of ideals to be pursued by the political, legal and economic system. For example, the principles include statements of upholding family values, including the statements that parents should support their children within or outside marriage until they reach the age of majority; that public bodies should promote and protect culture and should promote scientific research and development for the benefit of all; that all Spaniards should have the right to enjoy a dignified and adequate lifestyle; that public authorities should guarantee consumer protection by effective procedures so that consumers' health and safety and legitimate economic interests are covered; and that the old should be protected. These guiding principles have the characteristics of policy. Their vague terms allow them to be regarded as a meeting point between conservative and socialist ideology. Thus it might be possible to imagine that both political sides would support principles such as the aim to promote favourable conditions for social and economic progress, access to culture, science and research which would be of general social benefit, enrichment of historic culture and heritage and arts, well-being of the elderly, information and education for consumers, health and safety at work, and full employment. The differences between the two political sides would be manifested by the manner in which they sought to pursue these aims.

In summary, the first title of the constitution embraces and seeks to guarantee the freedoms for which Spanish people and Europeans have struggled since the origins of the liberal revolutions: the rights of man, political democracy, requiring at least that governors be elected by those they govern; the widening of the right of suffrage to include 18-year-olds; democratic control of public bodies; and procedural justice such as through the introduction of a jury in criminal procedure.

Titles II to IX set out the organizational structure of the state and define and state the duties of the relevant state organs of power, including the Crown, parliament, government, relations between government and parliament, and the judiciary. Included within this organizational section of the constitution are Title VII, which contains provisions for regulating economy and finance, Title VIII, which sets out the territorial organization of the state, providing general principles, and rules on local administration and the role and powers of the autonomous communities, and Title IX, which describes the constitutional court and its role and powers. These sections will be considered in detail in subsequent chapters of this book.

Title X deals with constitutional reform, which has been considered above. The remainder of the constitution consists of some additional and transitional provisions. The most important are the additional provisions relating to the territorial organization of the state. These provisions are followed by a derogation of those preconstitutional laws which oppose the provisions of the 1978 constitution. Under this derogation, the constitution will override prior laws where it seeks to have immediate effect, or to override other laws which contradict the constitution. The remaining laws will be left for the judgement of the constitutional court. The outcome of this derogation is that the only rupture with the previous legal system is where it cannot be interpreted in a way which is compatible with the new constitution. It is also necessary under this derogation to attempt all possible ways of interpretation before declaring a law invalid or unconstitutional. The final provision provides for the constitution to have immediate effect and orders the publication of the constitution in the other Spanish languages.

## Characteristics of the Constitution

The primary characteristics of the constitution are its moderate terms and its compromise nature. This is not surprising bearing in mind the context in which the constitution was created. Spain had, by then, become effectively a party political system dominated by two parties: the moderates and the socialists. The provisions also reflect a compromise of all the different views represented, although this was mainly dominated by the centre left and right views. The text suggests that the conservatives appeared to have accepted, at least formally, liberal democracy and a parliamentary monarchy as well as the political autonomy of the nationalities and regions and the possibility of a peaceful move towards socialism. The socialists appeared to have accepted a constitutional and legal approach to bringing about a classless society without exploitation. Piniella Sorli (1994) suggests that the political forces desired a constitutional pact above partisan positions. They sought a sociopolitical instrument that would be effective, pluralistic, flexible and lasting. This led to a constitution which reflects a compromise between the indissoluble unity of the Spanish nation and recognition of the right to autonomy of nationalities and regions, and between democracy, popular participation and the guarantee of freedom of enterprise within the framework of a market economy and subordination to the general interest of all types of wealth through an economic plan. Essentially, it is a constitution which sought neutrality or consensus as well as a balanced, mid-way position. It was a transaction between both ideological and institutional extremes.

The emphasis on principles and values in the constitution highlights at the same time another important characteristic: the tendency to submit to judicial control all relations of power, as much between entities and organs as between public bodies and citizens. This gives a strong role to the constitutional court and to the *Poder Judicial* and generates new tensions between the judicial organs and the political organs.

A significant weakness of the constitution is that it is an incomplete constitution, thereby relying on many supplementary laws and semi-constitutions of the autonomous communities to fill the gaps. However, the constitution is not just a source of production of law but is also a direct source of law and rights. It is applicable in itself and can stand up against any opposing legal rules. The constitution also acts as a framework by which to interpret other laws, since no law can be interpreted in isolation or independent of the constitution.

## References and Further Reading

Alzaga Villaamil, Oscar, Gutiérrez Gutiérrez, Ignacio and Rodríguez Zapata, Jorge, *Derecho Político Español Según La Constitución de 1978* (1997, Editorial Centro de Estudios, Madrid).
Cazorla Prieto Luís María and Arnaldo Alcubilla, Enrique, *Temas de Derecho Constitucional y Derecho Administrativo* (1988, Marcial Pons, Madrid).
Constitución Española (1978).
De Otto, Ignacio, *Derecho Constitucional – Sistema de Fuentes* (1993, Ariel, Barcelona).
González Casanova, J.A., *Teoría del Estado y Derecho Constitucional*, 3rd edn (1987, Vicens Universidad, Barcelona).
Heywood, Paul, *The Government and Politics of Spain* (1995, Macmillan, London).
López Guerra, Luís *et al.*, *Derecho Constitucional*, vol. I, 3rd edn (1997, Tirant lo Blanch, Valencia).
Piniella Sorli, Juan-Sebastián, *Sistema de Fuentes y Bloque de Constitucionalidad – Encrucijada de Competencias* (1994, Bosch, Barcelona).
Predieri, Alberto and García de Enterría, Eduardo, *La Constitución Española de 1978 – Estudios Sistemáticos* (1981, Civitas, Madrid).
Preston, Paul, *The Triumph of Democracy in Spain* (1986, Routledge, London).
Rubio Llorente, Francisco, *La Forma del Poder – Estudios Sobre La Constitución*, (1993, Centro de Estudios Constitucionales, Madrid).
Sánchez Agesta, Luís, *Curso de Derecho Constitucional Comparado* (1980, Universidad de Madrid, Madrid).

# 3     Institutions within the Constitution

The introduction to this book established that Spain has developed into a constitutional democracy. This has involved many fundamental changes to the organizational structure of the state. Spain has emerged into a parliamentary monarchy. The 1978 constitution also follows the classic principle of separation of powers, thus requiring not only a monarchy but other institutions such as a parliament, a government and a court system, each representing, respectively, the legislature, the executive and the judiciary. The constitution provides formally the role and powers of these institutions.

## The Crown

Article 1 of the constitution defines Spain as a parliamentary monarchy. This indicates that the king has an important constitutional role. In the negotiations for the constitution, the role of the king was an important part of the discussions. This is not surprising in the light of Spanish constitutional history during which the monarch had moved between having almost total political control to being denied any constitutional position during the republican periods. The political left preferred a merely symbolic king, and the right preferred a king to have a role similar to other European royals. The final draft of the constitution left the king with an intermediate position between those two models: a modern monarchy without political powers although without loss of its international role. As Olivan López *et al.* (1993) observe, the institution of the monarchy has a double justification. On the one hand, it gives continuity to the monarchic tradition and, on the other hand, the creators of the constitution would see the monarchy as a means of providing the unity and moderation necessary for achieving the transition to democracy. Thus the monarchy would serve as a reference point for all interested parties.

The role of the king is set out in Title II of the constitution. Article 56 states the general constitutional position of the king, while Article 62 defines the king's internal political role and Article 63 sets out his external functions. Article 56 states:

1. The King is the Chief of State, a symbol of the state's unity and stability, he arbitrates and moderates the activities of the institutions, and is regarded as the highest representative of Spain in international relations, especially with those nations connected with Spain's historical community, and exercises the functions given to him expressly by the Constitution and the laws.
2. The monarch's title is that of King of Spain and he shall be entitled to use other titles which correspond to the Crown.
3. The King's identity is inviolable and he is not subject to political responsibility. His acts shall be authorised in the form established in Article 64 and they will lack validity without such authority.

Article 56 establishes four main aspects to the king's role. First, he is a symbol of unity and permanence of the state. Thus, while political changes may occur in the parliament and government, the king remains constantly in his position. Secondly, he also has a role of moderating and arbitrating the regular functioning of the institutions. Thirdly, he must be kept informed of all affairs of the state. Fourthly, on an international level, the king represents the highest level of representation for the state. The king may also exercise functions expressly attributed to him by the constitution and other laws. These provisions make clear that the king has an important but limited role and one in which he acts as a symbol, an arbiter and a moderator.

## The King's Symbolic Role

As Article 56 provides, the symbolic role of the king is to act as chief of state with a character symbolizing the state's unity and permanence. To be a symbol of the state is not the same as personifying the state or adopting the sovereignty of the nation, but it means unity of the power of the state and the union between the state's organs. In this role the king promulgates the laws, convenes the parliamentary chambers, appoints the president of the government and members of the constitutional court, and justice is administered in the king's name. The king is not the supreme political power of the state. Rather, the acts of a state organ are regarded as acts of the state. It is not that the king should have the specific function of unifying the state or its powers, but that he has the other function of representing or symbolizing unity.

The concrete functions that correspond to the king and his symbolic character concern the king's international role, his relationship with the armed forces, his cultural position and his position in connection with the administration of justice. At an international level, the king assumes the highest representative position in Spanish international relations. The reality of this position, however, is that the king does not intervene in every case but only in the honouring and reception of ambassadors and of heads of diplomatic missions or permanent missions before international or Spanish organizations. Nor does the king's international role endow him with decision-making powers in external politics. In this way the constitution is careful to contain conditions on the activities of the king which require prior authorization from the *Cortes Generales*, such as a declaration of war and signing a peace treaty. With regard to the armed forces, the king has the supreme mandate of the armed forces, although the direction of external policies and defence policy is within the competence of the government and the military administration. In reality, the king is limited to formalizing acts of the person authorized to act: the president of the government or the Ministry of Defence. In connection with cultural matters, the king is the chief patron of the royal academies and he gives concessions for employment, honours and distinctions. These represent the classic functions of chiefs of state. In the sphere of administration of justice, justice is exercised in the name of the king and he exercises the right of granting grace. However, the king cannot exercise this right against the government.

*The King as Moderator*

As a moderator the king prevents any oppressive actions by the constitutional institutions, including his own. Thus the king does not exercise more functions than those attributed to him by the constitution or by the laws. This moderating power and harmonizing role can be said to describe the king as reigning without governing. His function as moderator is more that of a role of influence over the activities of the constitutional organs. In this role the king exercises the function of sanctioning laws created by the parliamentary bodies. Traditionally, the king gave his agreement to and acceptance of the contents of a text, but the legislative powers now reside only in the *Cortes*. 'Sanction' may be distinguished from 'veto', so that the king merely formalizes the laws rather than saying whether or not he accepts them. In this way, the king merely expedites legislative decrees and puts them forward for publication. Another aspect of the king's moderating role is that he must be informed of the matters of state. Being informed about state matters is an obligation of the state authorities and in particular of the government. Consequently, the king can preside over sessions of the council of ministers when he considers it appropriate, such as at the request of the president of the government. The king also convenes elections, and appoints and dismisses the president of the government and ministers, and he convenes and dissolves the *Cortes*.

## The Arbitral Role of the King

The king may have to intervene in the affairs of institutions where there appears to be a constitutional dispute. The authority and influence of the monarchy may be useful at a time when delicate political situations need to be resolved. In reality, the only occasion on which the king may have to mediate between the executive and the legislature is that of his proposal of candidate for president of the government. In this situation the king has a certain key role of leadership and even a margin of discretion, principally when the election result has not been clearly favourable to one of the political forces.

Another aspect of the provisions of Article 56 is the absence of political responsibility of the king. This is an old privilege and, according to Article 56.3, the king is not politically accountable and the acts of royalty thus do not require authority for giving them validity. In reality, however, the political acts of the king are not his own but are the acts of the government and the *Cortes* and consequently they need to be authorized. The requirement of authority can be regarded as a material limitation of the royal power because the authorizing person or body assumes responsibility entirely. Indeed, because the king is said to have no responsibility, he cannot act alone but must always act with the agreement of another organ. Normally, it is the president of the government or the competent minister or the president of the congress of deputies who may provide this authority. Such authority may be expressed or implied. Almost all royal actions require authority and those acts which do not need to be authorized concern the private life of the king: the distribution of the Crown's dowry and the appointment of the civil and military members of the royal household. In reality the authorized acts are acts of another organ to which the king gives his approval, endowing it with the status of an official act. For example, although they are deemed to be in the king's name, the appointment and dismissal of ministers are proposed by the president of the government and legislative decrees are approved in the council of ministers, and in these acts resides the total responsibility of the authorizer.

In reality, the royal powers in nearly all their aspects remain very limited and the king's functions are never totally independent. Normally, he acts together with other institutions, either with their approval or with their authority. His acts are not party political but he has influence and thus ought to be as neutral as possible. It is this neutrality which enables the king to gain the confidence of the public. This also enables him to have great influence with few powers. Thus, although the king's powers are limited to the extent that his function is more ceremonial and symbolic, this fact also endows the monarchy with strength and stability. Its prestige arises from its lack of real and effective powers. While Article 62 provides the king with various functions (rather than powers) these functions are to be regulated by other provisions in the constitution or by other laws. The king's functions can be divided also into legislative, executive and judicial functions. For example, his legislative functions include sanctioning and promulgating laws, and convening the parliament and elections and referendums. His executive functions include proposing and appointing the president and ministers of the government, and expediting decrees of the council of ministers. His judicial functions include the granting of grace.

In practice, the constitutional provisions leave the king reduced to a symbolic and almost decorative figure. Yet any extraordinary event highlights his unifying and stabilizing role over the democratic system. A good illustration of his authority was seen during the attempted military coup in 1981 when, as head of the armed forces, the king refused to sanction the attempted military dictatorship. The king is also a very good ambassador for Spain. He has managed to integrate Spain into an important nation in international relations, particularly in Spain's entry into the European Community, as well as in Spain's relations with Latin America.

In conclusion, the role of the monarchy is relatively weak in theory but in practice has been shown to be important and strong.

## The *Cortes Generales*

The *Cortes Generales* are the parliamentary chambers. Their role and functions are provided in Title III of the constitution. Article 66 defines them as follows: they represent the Spanish people and comprise the congress of deputies and the senate. The *Cortes Generales* exercise the legislative powers of the state, approve its taxes, and control government. Effectively, the *Cortes Generales* are regarded as the supreme representative organ.

As is noted by Cazorla Prieto and Arnaldo Alcubilla (1988), both chambers have a representative function, a deliberative character, are inviolable, act publicly and demonstrate political supremacy. The representative function of the two chambers is such that they are each elected by the Spanish people. This public election of the *Cortes Generales* is linked to Article 23 of the constitution, which provides a right for citizens to participate in politics. Similarly, under Article 68, all persons who have the right to vote also have the right to stand for election to the congress of deputies. Thus, under Article 68, the congress of deputies represents the people generally, while, under Article 69, the senate represents people in regional and territorial matters. This territorial representation derives from the recognition and protection of autonomy of nationalities and regions provided in Article 2. The congress of deputies, which is directly elected, is constituted by proportional representation, while the senate is partly directly elected by a first-past-the-post system, and partly selected by the assemblies of each autonomous community according to the size and political composition of that community, by a system of proportional representation.

Their deliberative role means that each chamber must consider legislative proposals within a fixed time. The constitution fixes the time periods for considering and approving such proposals and establishes means by which an agreement can be reached where there is initially disagreement between the chambers. The constitution therefore designates the *Cortes* as the place for open discussions of the arguments for and against a legislative proposal so that laws are created by rational methods. In this way, all parliamentary decisions are taken after debate or consideration by the *Cortes*. The principle of inviolability, which is provided in Article 66.3, suggests that the *Cortes* have no responsibility. However, they can be politically responsible, so that, for example, if the congress does not comply with its mission to elect a president, the chambers may be dissolved. The constitutional court may also declare a law approved by the *Cortes* as unconstitutional, which may have the effect of striking down the law created in the parliament. The *Cortes* bring to the parliament some stability with the institution of the *Diputación Permanente*. This institution offers a guarantee of permanency necessary for achieving an overall balance and stability in the constitutional system. The *Cortes* act publicly and therefore the sessions of the two chambers are held in public. This is regarded as important for the representation of the people. The parliament is also the source of primary decisions and, because it is elected by the people, it represents the concept of popular sovereignty.

As has been noted, the *Cortes Generales* have a bicameral structure based on the existence of the congress of deputies and the senate. This is indicative of a pluralist society as well as a recognition of the need to represent the regions whose autonomy is provided for by the constitution. In this way, the senate has a role of territorial representation. It represents the autonomous communities but it has a very limited role in so far as it is much smaller than the congress of deputies and the constitution does not confer special functions on the senate in relation to the autonomous communities. The main role of the senate is to protect the autonomous communities against centralist tendencies of the congress.

Although the congress is technically the lower chamber, the reality is that it has the stronger position. Indeed, the bicameral structure is not regarded as an equal bicameralism. Thus the congress, for example, may within certain time limits raise a veto of the senate and may approve or reject amendments introduced by the senate. The congress is also the place where the law-making process is initiated. Only the congress may pronounce the approval of decree-laws (*Decretos-leyes*). It is the congress which will bring charges of treason or offences against the security of the state by the president or other members of the government. The congress may authorize a consultative referendum requested by the president of the government. Where there is a situation of emergency, the congress dominates.

Under Article 68 of the constitution, as well as under the Organic Law of the General Electoral System, the congress has 300–400 deputies elected by universal suffrage for a period of four years and created by a system of proportional representation. The senate is also elected for four years and from each province four senators are elected. The autonomous communities will designate a senator and one more person for every million inhabitants within the territory.

The two chambers each have their own set of internal regulations and these are regarded as the supreme legal source in this area. Under Article 72.1 of the constitution, the chambers may establish their own regulations, and the regulations and their reform would be subject to a final vote requiring approval by an absolute majority. These regulations are susceptible to scrutiny by the constitutional court as regards their constitutionality. The regulations cover procedures and modes of action by the chambers; their organs and functions; the relations between these organs and other state organs, and in particular with the government; the parliamentary statutes; and rules of functioning.

Generally, the functions of the *Cortes Generales* are to create legislation and to control government action. Both chambers participate in the creation of legislation which is provided in Article 90 of the constitution. As for control of the executive, Article 108 of the constitution provides that the government responds to the congress of deputies. For example, the government must submit itself to parliamentary questions. The congress may also decide on the question of confidence in the government and has a power of a motion of censure. As the parliament functions through bicameralism, it comes as no surprise that the two chambers should have different functions. Thus the senate prevails over matters concerning the autonomous communities, while the congress of deputies dominates other matters.

The parliamentary sessions, according to Article 73.1 of the constitution, run from September to December and from February to June. They may also meet for extraordinary sessions and, occasionally, the chambers can hold joint sessions: for example, for non-legislative matters which concern the Crown, or to provide for a successor to the Crown, or to authorize or prohibit the marriage of the successor to the Crown, or for approval of state ratification of an international treaty which requires approval by absolute majority of each chamber.

Each chamber has its own president and each chamber has a directorate which directs the organization of the work and the regime and internal government of that chamber. The directorate plans the general activities of the chamber and fixes a timetable for the activities of the full chamber and the commissions established by the chamber. It also formalizes parliamentary documents. Each chamber also has a *Junta de Portavoces*, a board on which there are representative spokespersons of each parliamentary group and through which occurs a dialogue between the majority and the opposition. This *Junta de Portavoces* is therefore a mediator or facilitator of compromises. Each chamber also has functional organs by which the work of the chamber is carried out. These organs consist of the *Pleno*, which is a meeting of all the members of the chamber and which ensures unity of the parliamentray work and reflects parliamentary sovereignty. Other functional organs are the parliamentary commissions which prepare and develop the legislative work and then pass their decisions on to the *Pleno* for discussion. The commissions also set up their own *Ponencias* which provide a report or proposal and the commissions may be either permanent legislative or permanent non-legislative or temporary commissions established by the *Ponencia* at the request of the *Pleno*. Each chamber also has a permanent deputation, comprising 21 members on the basis of proportional representation and with the function of maintaining continuity for the relevant chamber. Each chamber also has parliamentary groups which are organized politically and discuss policy issues. Finally, the administration of each chamber is presided over by a general secretary. The functioning of the chambers focuses on the convening of meetings, the timetabling of activities, general rules of debate, a quorum and forms of voting.

In summary, today the parliament is the place for meeting, agreeing and negotiating policy and is a platform from which to explain to the country the positions of the political parties with regard to their policies. It might be improved by establishing more speedy procedures.

## The Government

Title IV of the constitution regulates the government and administration, although within this title the government and administration are treated separately. Article 97 provides that 'the Government directs internal and external policy, civil and military administration and national defence. It exercises an executive function and has regulatory power in accordance with the Constitution and the law'. Thus, from this article, we can see that the government has an executive and policy-making function. In Spanish constitutional history, the government is a relatively recent institution, with the executive powers having previously been within the Crown's domain. Still today the Spanish government is the king's government, but in reality it acts in its own capacity. Article 97 also makes it clear that the government is the chief political organ as well as being the head of the civil and military administration, and it has regulatory powers.

The government's political functions include creating the political programme and initiation and execution of the general state budget and economic planning. The government also has the power of legislative initiative. Additionally, it may exercise arbitral functions such as dissolution of the chambers or the calling of a consultative referendum. Another task for the government is defence and direction of the military administration. Finally, the government directs external policies, including initiatives in treaties and conventions.

The government is formed by appointment of a president. The king proposes a candidate after prior consultation with delegates of the political groups which are represented in parliament and the president of the congress of deputies. The chosen candidate outlines the political programme of the government that he intends to pursue and asks for the confidence of the congress of deputies. This programme is a personal declaration of the president's political intentions. If the congress of deputies gives by absolute majority its approval to the candidate, the king then appoints him as president. If he does not achieve an absolute majority then, 48 hours later, there is another vote and he can be accepted by a simple majority. If he does not obtain a simple majority then a new proposal is proceeded with. Other members of the government are appointed and dismissed by the king at the proposal of the president. It is important to note, therefore, that the king appoints but does not choose. The government closes down after general elections take place and when it loses parliamentary confidence. It may also close for reasons provided in the constitution or as a result of illness or death of the president.

The government's structure is collegiate, comprising the president, one or more vice-presidents, ministers and other members as established by law. The role of the president of the government is provided in Article 98.2 of the constitution, which states that the president directs the action of the government and coordinates the functions of the other members of the government without prejudice to their competence and direct responsibility in the course of their business. By contrast with Article 97, this article seeks, not to specify the government's competences, but to fix the internal relations between the president and the members of the government. It seeks to obtain a balance between a predominant leader and a collective ideal.

The government itself is subject to legal regulation and control. Thus, if any individuals are injured or their interests are adversely affected by government action, they may be compensated.

## The Relationship between the Government and the Cortes Generales

Cazorla Prieto and Arnaldo Alcubilla (1988) state that a fundamental element of the parliamentary system is that there is a functional link between the legislature and the executive. The characteristic of this link is that the legislature controls the political activity of the executive. The government requires the confidence of the parliament in order to carry out its activities. In this way the parliament has both a legislative function and a controlling function.

Title V of the constitution provides for a system which aims to guarantee to the executive as much stability as possible, by reinforcing the principle of unity and cohesion of the executive as well as unity in the direction of state policy. In this way, under Article 108, the government must answer collectively to the congress of deputies with regard to its political activities. Under Article 109, the parliament and its commissions shall be able to obtain information and assistance from the government and governmental departments and from whichever other authorities of the state or the autonomous communities apply. The parliament, as provided by Article 110, can call upon the members of the government to come before it. The government may also attend parliamentary sessions and may make itself heard.

The government's political responsibility before the congress of deputies is demonstrated in two ways: first, the parliament may refuse to express confidence in the government; secondly, it may approve of a motion of censure. Under Article 112 of the constitution, the president of the government, after discussion in the council of ministers, may present to the congress of deputies the question of confidence over its programme or over a declaration of general policy. The government may consider that confidence has been granted if a simple majority of the deputies votes in favour of the programme or policy. Under Article 113, the congress of deputies may by absolute majority adopt a motion of censure. The motion of censure shall be proposed by at least a tenth of the deputies and must include a candidate for the presidency of the government. After five days a vote is taken. If those asking for a censure fail to achieve enough votes, they shall not be able to call for another censure during that period of parliamentary sessions.

If the congress withdraws confidence in the government, the congress will present this to the king and proceed to appoint a new president following the procedure set out in Article 99 of the constitution. Similarly, if the congress adopts a motion of censure, that will be presented to the king and the candidate included in the motion will be deemed to have been invested with the confidence of the chamber and Article 99 shall be invoked. The king will then appoint the president of the government. The dissolution of the government at its own initiative may be a third route but this is not conclusive. If the government's dissolution is initiated by the *Cortes Generales*, this may originate from various motives, for example loss of a vote that is considered important for the government.

Confidence is described by Cazorla Prieto and Arnaldo Alcubilla (1988) as a suicide threat by the government. The confidence of the parliament in the government serves to enable the government to rely on the parliament which has to carry out its programme and to bring it up to date or to reform it. Confidence also serves to allow the government to face any opposition by one parliamentary chamber in relation to a political decision that the government considers essential for its business. In reality, only the majority group of the opposition will be able to introduce a motion of censure; the minority groups may only be able to do so through agreement among themselves.

While the government may be dissolved at the initiative of the congress of deputies, so also can the government propose the dissolution of the congress, or the senate or the parliament. This will be decreed by the king. This possibility seeks to ensure equilibrium between the government and the parliament. It was originally a prerogative of the monarchy, but now the proposal of dissolution of the parliament or one of the parliamentary chambers is regarded as a mode of resolving conflicts between the government and the parliament. The government will not be able to make such a proposal once a process of motion of censure has begun.

Another aspect of parliamentary control is that the parliament may examine the activity of the government. It exercises control by means of authorization of government acts such as signing or ratifying international treaties or initiating a consultative referendum. Parliament also exercises control by inspection, such as by questions, interrogatories and motions. By a question the parliament can be informed or obtain clarification upon the activity of the government or the administration. Interrogatories are acts by which the parliament can request an explanation of matters concerning general policy either from the government or from the ministerial department. Motions are acts by which a parliamentary chamber may express its position on a determined question but without any binding legal effects.

## *El Poder Judicial*

The explanatory memorandum of the *Ley Orgánica del Poder Judicial* defines the *Poder Judicial* as the group of organs that are charged by the constitution with exclusive power of jurisdiction in all processes of judging and enforcing judgments.

Article 117.1 of the constitution states that justice emanates from the people and is administered in the name of the king by judges and magistrates who are part of the *Poder Judicial*. Article 117.2 provides further that judges and magistrates shall not be dismissed, removed or retired except for a cause and with the guarantees provided in the law. Judges gain their competences by jurisdictional orders in branches of the law. Within each order or branch of law the judicial organs are granted certain powers for the issue which may be tried. Some of their powers may also be determined by the law of the place where the incident to be judged occurred.

The principles of jurisdiction include independence, stability, responsibility, exclusivity, unity, submission to the law and good faith. The principle of independence means independence with respect to all citizens and all public bodies. Independence is relevant not only against individuals and other public bodies but also against other judicial bodies. The principle of stability means that, in accordance with Article 117.2 of the constitution, judges and magistrates cannot be dismissed, suspended, transferred or retired. The principle of responsibility confirms that judges and magistrates have penal, civil and disciplinary responsibility. Exclusivity means that judges' and magistrates' jurisdictional competences are determined by laws and international treaties, and judges and magistrates may not exercise more functions than those expressly provided. Unity means that jurisdiction is unique and is exercised by the judges and courts as prescribed by the law. This unity does not prevent judicial organs being given specific competences within each branch of the law. In this regard, the following jurisdictions exist: civil law, criminal law, social law and administrative law. The principle of submission to the law means that judges and magistrates are only subject to the law. They are bound to the constitution which represents the supreme or primary or highest rule of the legal system. Judges and courts must protect the rights and legitimate interests as much of individuals as of collective bodies. Judges and courts shall not apply the rules or other provisions in a way which contradicts the constitution or the law or the principle of legal hierarchy. With regard to the principle of good faith, Article 11 of the *Ley Orgánica del Poder Judicial* states that all procedures shall respect the rules of good faith. Consequently, judicial procedures shall not contravene fundamental liberties. Additionally, the judges and courts must reject petitions, incidents and exceptions that are formulated in order to abuse the law or to commit fraud of law or process.

Article 119 of the constitution provides that justice shall be administered free when the law so states and shall always be granted free to those who do not have sufficient means for the expenses of litigation. Under Article 120 of the constitution, judicial activities will be conducted in public except where the law provides otherwise, and shall be conducted orally, especially in criminal trials, and decisions shall be delivered before a public audience.

## Institutions of the Poder Judicial

*The Consejo General del Poder Judicial*   Under Article 122 of the constitution, the *Consejo General del Poder Judicial* governs the *Poder Judicial*. It is a national organ, its basic function being the appointment of judges and magistrates and inspection of judicial and court activities, operating also as a disciplinary system. The *Consejo General* also makes known certain plans for legal reform and proposals by magistrates of the constitutional court. The *Consejo General* consists of the president of the Supreme Court – who, at the same time, is the president of the council – and 20 other members. Those other members are appointed by the king for a period of five years after being nominated by the congress of deputies or by the senate.

*The Supreme Court*   The Supreme Court is, according to Article 123, the highest court, apart from the Constitutional Court which is the highest court relating to constitutional matters. The Supreme Court's geographical jurisdiction covers the whole of Spain and sits in Madrid. Its President shall be appointed by the King, at the proposal of the *Consejo General*.

*The fiscal ministry*   The fiscal ministry is a state organ with the role of promoting justice to protect the rights of citizens and of the public interest. The functions of the fiscal ministry are regulated by the organic statute of the fiscal ministry.

*The constitutional court*   The constitutional court is a national court and is the highest-level interpreter of the constitution. Its remit is to guarantee respect for the constitution by other institutions and organs of the state, and thereby to act as a guarantor of respect for the fundamental rights and public liberties provided by the constitution. The constitutional court is composed of 12 members appointed by the king. Four members are proposed by the congress, four by the senate, two by the *Consejo General del Poder Judicial* and two are proposed by the government. Normally, the members of the constitutional court are magistrates and fiscals, university professors, civil servants and lawyers with more than 15 years of professional experience. They are appointed for a period of nine years. During their appointment they cannot have public or administrative duties. Nor may they have directive functions in the political parties or union associations, or carry out professional or commercial activities. The prerogatives of the members of the constitutional court are independence, inviolability and stability, and they have only criminal legal responsibility.

The constitutional court has the following competences: declaration of unconstitutionality against laws and provisions that are meant to have legal force, for example statutes of autonomy, international treaties and regulations of the chambers of the *Cortes Generales* and the *Consejo General*. The court seeks to protect all citizens against violations of their fundamental rights and civil liberties caused by legal provisions and legal acts or by actions of public bodies or civil servants. The court deals with constitutional conflicts: for example, conflicts between the state and the autonomous communities or between the autonomous communities themselves, or conflicts between the constitutional institutions.

The case load of the constitutional court has increased considerably since 1980: between 1980 and 1986, it dealt with 730 cases; in 1988, it had 2268 cases, and in 1993 it decided 3982 cases. Consequently, there are now considerable delays, with cases taking up to two and a half years to be resolved.

*Tribunales superiores de Justicia*   These have competence over the judicial organization of the autonomous communities and correspond to the division of powers at a regional level. They may judge on petitions against territorial laws and are empowered to resolve electoral conflicts. Where the courts commit an error of law or a procedural error in the administration of justice, the state will be responsible for compensating for harm or damage which may arise out of those errors.

Article 125 of the constitution provides for citizen participation in the judicial system by way of jury participation. In 1995, a new law regulating the jury system was established.

## References and Further Reading

Asensi Sabater, José, *Constitucionalismo y Derecho Constitucional – Materias Para Una Introducción* (1996, Tirant lo Blanch, Valencia).

Casey, James, 'The Spanish Constitutional Court' (1990–92), *Irish Jurist*, 26–56.

Cazorla Prieto, Luís María and Arnaldo Alcubilla, Enrique, *Temas de Derecho Constitucional y Derecho Administrativo* (1988, Marcial Pons, Madrid).

Cotarelo, Ramon, 'La Jefatura del Estado', in Francisco J. Bobillo (ed.), *España a Debate – La Política* (1991, Tecnos, Madrid), pp. 1–13.

Herrero, Miguel and de Minón, R., 'La Posición Constitucional de la Corona', in various authors (eds), *Estudios Sobre la Constitución Española – Homenaje a Profesor Eduardo García de Enterría* (1991, Civitas, Madrid).

López Guerra, Luís *et al.*, *Derecho Constitucional*, vol. II, 3rd edn (1997, Tirant lo Blanch, Valencia).

Olivan López, Fernando *et al.*, Introducción al Derecho, 3rd edn (1993, Tecnos, Madrid).

Rubio Llorente, Francisco, *La Forma del Poder* (1993, Centro de Estudios Constitucionales, Madrid), esp. pp. 265–79, 409–62.

Torres del Moral, Antonio, *Principios de Derecho Constitucional Español* (1986, Atom, Madrid).

# 4    The Sources of Law

One of the primary characteristics of Spanish law is the existence of its codes: the Civil Code, the Commercial Code and the Criminal Code. During the nineteenth century, following the example of the French legal system, the Civil Code of 1889 was created after several attempts. This code has a very important role in the systematization of the law and how the law is arranged and organized. In particular, the first title in the Civil Code contains provisions relating to the system of sources of the Spanish legal system. In Spain, the term 'sources of law' has two possible meanings. First, the term may be understood as the sources of production of the law, such as by whom or by which body a law is created. The second possible significance refers to the laws themselves and the sources of legal knowledge such as the jurisprudence (case law) or doctrine which interprets the rules. The sources of law, then, are the place or person by which the laws are created as well as the laws themselves.

Spain follows the continental tradition by which written laws take priority, unlike the situation in the common law systems whereby the case law and precedent are an important part of the law.

## The Hierarchy of Laws

The Civil Code, in its Article 6, required judges to apply custom in the absence of a written law and, failing that, to apply general principles of law. In 1974, a decree introduced into the Civil Code a preliminary title with the heading 'On legal norms, their application and use'. The preliminary title contains rules on the application of laws, establishing rules of interpretation, equity and analogy as well as the temporal, territorial and personal use of the relevant rules. The preliminary title is thus a group of rules concerned with the sources of law, and their application and interpretation. This makes up a common law system which is supplemented by the constitutional law, with specific rules relevant to individual sectors within the legal system, in particular those relating to administrative law, fiscal, criminal and labour law.

The Spanish Civil Code defines the only recognized sources. The primary sources are the *Ley* (broadly encompassing written legislation), custom and general principles of law. Jurisprudence (in the sense of case law) is regarded as a secondary source. Article 1(2) of the code sets out a hierarchy to deprive of validity those provisions that contradict a superior rule within the hierarchy. The code also sets out the technical relationship between the different classes of sources within the hierarchical framework. This hierarchy of laws is expressly recognized in Article 9(3) of the Spanish Constitution.

The legal hierarchy is a vertical hierarchy by which, as has just been noted, certain rules cannot contradict those above them in the hierarchy. Conversely, the rules at a higher level in the hierarchy may override rules lower down the hierarchy. The hierarchy established in the Civil Code consists of the following order of priority of rules: laws, custom, general principles of law. Within the top layer of rules, the laws, there is another hierarchy. For example, a *ley orgánica* cannot be contradicted by a *reglamento* – an administrative regulation (as described below). If a *reglamento* is created which contradicts a *ley*, this will be null. Further, if a *ley* is created after a *reglamento* and contradicts the *reglamento*, the effect will be to derogate or destroy the *reglamento*: it will no longer have legal effect.

## The *Ley*

The *ley* is regarded as the principal source of Spanish law. It is a superior norm which is given preference over other legal rules and is established with the maximum of formalities in order to provide with authority the *ley* and the organ to whom is reserved competence for its creation.

There are several different classes of *leyes*. Indeed, there is no exhaustive list. The Spanish Constitution of 1978 is the most important: the so-called 'basic norm'. After the constitution, the next in order of significance are the *leyes orgánicas* and the *leyes ordinarias*. Organic laws refer to the development of fundamental rights and civil liberties. For example, there exist organic laws which give formal approval to the statutes of autonomy and the electoral regime and other systems provided in the constitution. *Leyes ordinarias* deal with any issue outside those covered by a *ley orgánica*. *Decretos legislativos* are provisions made by the government which contain delegated legislation. *Decretos leyes* are unusual measures for urgent situations and are really provisional legislative measures. *Leyes de transferencia y delegación*, *leyes marco* and *leyes de armonisación* all refer to matters within the competence of the autonomous communities. Following these comes legislation of the autonomous communities. The final level within the category of *leyes* is that of administrative rules such as decrees and ministerial orders.

There is a *ley* in the wide sense and a *ley* in the narrow sense. In its wide sense, a *ley* is every written legal rule, while in the strict sense it is every written rule created by parliament. These two senses of *ley* are recognized and distinguished by the Supreme Court in the following way: the word *ley* can be understood in a restricted form as an order created by the sovereign organs which are constitutionally attributed with superior legislative power, whereas, in its substantive form, all written legal rules such as decrees which are general and impose obligations may be regarded as a *ley*. Whichever approach is adopted may have implications for an individual, since to consider the *ley* in its wider sense means potentially that an administrative body, which might be unelected, could effectively create a *ley* that, strictly speaking, would override a contrary custom in the hierarchy of legal rules.

## Classes of Laws

*Laws in the strict sense*   The strict approach regards *leyes* as those which are created by the parliament and possibly delegated legislation in the form of decrees which are not created by the parliament but by the government.

At the top of the hierarchy is found the constitution, which is regarded as the supreme *ley*. All other laws must be adapted to coincide with the constitution. Any laws or rules which are contrary to the provisions in the constitution are void and, equally, all prior laws which do not agree with the constitution are overridden by the constitution and lose their legal force from the date on which the constitution entered into force.

*Leyes orgánicas*   According to Article 81 of the constitution, *leyes orgánicas* are those laws which develop fundamental rights and civil liberties, those which are given approval in the statutes of autonomy and the general electoral regime and those provided for in the constitution. In a sense, certain matters are reserved for an organic law and those are contained in the constitution. The *ley orgánica* effectively develops the principles set out in the constitution. It is possible for the *ley orgánica* to remit certain matters to a *ley ordinaria*, so that there may exist a collaboration between different rules. Alternatively, certain matters could be left to delegated legislation. In order to obtain approval for the *leyes orgánicas* an absolute majority in the congress is required.

*Leyes ordinarias*   A *ley ordinaria* is defined as a written rule created by the legislative body: the *Cortes Generales*. *Leyes ordinarias* must be created and voted on and approved by the *Cortes Generales*. Some may be approved by a parliamentary commission, others by the *pleno* – full meeting of the two chambers – to which are reserved matters involving reform of the constitution, international questions, *leyes orgánicas* and *leyes de bases* – laws which set out the guidelines for subsequent laws on the specified topic – and the state general budgets. Legal doctrine suggests that the *ley ordinaria* may deal with any issue outside of those reserved for the *ley orgánica*. More specifically, the constitution makes reference in some of its provisions to matters, such as budgetary matters, military obligations, taxes, marriage, labour relations, the professional colleges, collective bargaining and protection of public health, which ought to be regulated by means of a *ley*. Basically, for these issues the general principles should be set out in a *ley*, but their details should be developed further by administrative rules or regulations.

Other *leyes ordinarias* are those created by the parliaments of the autonomous communities on those subjects and in conformity with their statutes in which they have competence to dictate rules by means of a *ley*. These *leyes* will be applicable only in the relevant territory of that autonomous community.

*Leyes orgánicas* and *leyes ordinarias* have the same hierarchical status. The only differences between them are the subject matter with which they may deal and the procedure used to create them. A *ley ordinaria* which purports to cover those matters identified in Article 81 of the constitution would be declared as unconstitutional because those matters are reserved for *leyes orgánicas*. On the other hand, a *ley orgánica* which deals with areas other than those listed in Article 81 is likely to be treated as a *ley ordinaria*.

*International treaties*   These are also *leyes* and, following the monist system, they automatically become part of Spanish law once they are signed and ratified, without requiring further legislative implementation. The constitution identifies three types of treaties. First, Article 93 refers to treaties which confer some of the powers of the state on an international organization and these require a prior *ley orgánica* to authorize the signing of the treaty. The second type of treaty requires prior authorization by parliament through an agreement of both chambers sitting at the request of the executive. These treaties are political in nature and may affect fundamental rights and liberties or create obligations on the state. Other treaties may be signed and ratified by the executive which needs only to inform the parliament after the treaty has been ratified. Generally, treaties have a subordinate position to the constitution and so if a treaty contradicts the constitution it will be necessary to alter the constitution before signing and ratifying the treaty. Alternatively, the constitutional court may declare that the treaty or some parts of it are unconstitutional and therefore inapplicable.

Generally, the legislative power for creating *leyes* is restricted to the *Cortes Generales*, while the government has only the power to develop those laws and to create regulations. However, it is possible for the government to create a limited form of legislation by way of *decretos leyes* and delegated legislation known as *decretos legislativos*.

*Decretos leyes*   These are created when there is a situation of urgency and need. In this situation the executive may, under Article 86.1, introduce provisional rules which have the force of law. It is therefore necessary to place a number of limitations on this power of the executive. Thus the *decreto ley* may not affect the organization of the basic institutions of the state, the fundamental rights and civil liberties, the organization and powers of the autonomous communities or the general electoral regime.

The *decreto ley* must be approved by the *Cortes* who have the power to create legislation. Thus Article 86.3 of the constitution states that the *decretos leyes* must immediately be submitted to a debate and a vote of the whole congress of deputies, within the time limit of 30 days following its promulgation. Within 30 days, the congress should state expressly its approval or rejection of the *decreto ley*. If congress approves the law it can be converted into an ordinary *ley* by an expedited procedure. It appears that a decision of the constitutional court has had the effect of giving to such converted *leyes* retrospective effect, which is contrary to Article 9(3) of the constitution.

*Decretos legislativos*   These are a form of delegated legislation by which parliament delegates its legislative power to the executive, made possible by Article 82 of the constitution. The parliament fixes the principles, criteria, object limits and scope of the delegation into a *ley de bases*. Alternatively, the parliament may grant to the executive the power to consolidate existing legislation. Here the executive's powers are limited to consolidation of existing rules only, and cannot introduce new rules. It is not possible for the parliament to delegate to the government powers of legislation for subjects which are the concern of *leyes orgánicas*. Thus the parliament cannot delegate on matters relating to fundamental rights and civil liberties, the statutes of autonomy, the general electoral regime, or anything else which would be considered as developing the constitution.

*Decretos legislativos*, while being created by the government, have the force and character of a *ley*. The classes of delegated legislation fall into two main categories: *textos articulados* and *textos refundidos*. *Textos articulados* are requested by the parliament from the government by means of a *ley de bases* which determines the limits of the delegation by defining precisely the object of legislation and the level of the legislative delegation as well as the principles and criteria that must be followed by the government in the exercise of its delegated power. In this way the *ley de bases* is limited to establishing the criteria and basic principles and elements of the future legal rule and the government is limited to developing such principles and criteria within the object and level determined in the *ley de bases* – the law of delegation of powers. *Textos refundidos* are rules created by government as a result of delegation whose aim is to reorganize various laws which regulate distinct aspects of the same matter into one single law – rather like a consolidating law. In this case the delegating law is produced by means of a *ley ordinaria*. The authorization of the parliament which provides the delegation must specify what is to be reorganized or consolidated, indicating the laws that are relevant.

Delegated legislation is to be regarded as an exception to the normal rule since it entails giving to the government a power which it does not ordinarily possess. Delegated legislation also involves a risk that the government will abuse this power and go beyond the boundary of its delegation. Consequently, the constitution places limits or requirements on the delegated legislation which may be regarded as a form of control on the government's activities. Thus the delegation must be granted to the government expressly for a specific matter and with a time limit in which the power may be exercised. The delegation must be publicized. The government may not subdelegate the power to non-governmental authorities.

*Reglamentos, decretos and other administrative provisions, all of which are inferior to the ley*   A *reglamento* (regulation) is a rule created by the public administration or by the executive. While the parliament has a legislative mandate, the government has regulatory powers under Article 97 of the constitution. In this way the state administration is able to create legal rules of a general or particular nature. The executive may pass *reglamentos* under Article 97 of the constitution, as may other state bodies, such as the *Consejo General del Poder Judicial* and the constitutional court, as well as the autonomous communities. In either case, the regulations are regarded technically as inferior in the legal hierarchy to the *leyes* and must therefore submit to the principles of legality and normative hierarchy. Thus a *reglamento* is subject to the *ley* and must not contradict the *ley*: it will be void if it contradicts the *ley*. *Reglamentos* may be independent or executory, the latter being *reglamentos* which develop an existing law. A *reglamento* may be created to establish the rules which govern the relationship between the administration and those subject to administration. The *reglamento* has the following characteristics: it is a rule of a general character in so far as it creates obligations to be complied with by everyone, it is an instrument of collaboration between the government and the legislature, and is an instrument of participation of the government in the organization of society.

The *decreto* is an administrative rule created by the government or by delegated commissions of the government.

## Custom

A custom has three fundamental characteristics: it is a source independent of the law; it does not need recognition of the law; it is a subsidiary source whose role is to fill possible gaps left by the laws. It is probably difficult to apply a custom since it is necessary to prove that it exists. Generally, customs are non-written laws, although it is possible for them to be in writing. Customary laws originate from society rather than from the state. It must also be shown that the custom is in use and this is likely to require evidence of more than one occasion on which it was used. There must also exist a general opinion about the obligation created by the custom.

Custom is developed independently of any other sources, and applies only where there is no existing written rule on the matter and it must be pleaded and proved before the court.

## General Principles of the Law

General principles of law are non-specific rules which are not formulated. They are more abstract and may be regarded as extrapositive principles. In this sense they are supplementary sources in the absence of law or custom and they have an informative role. In other words, general principles are used teleologically in so far as they are an instrument of interpretation for the rest of the legal rules. The general principles consist of values such as equality, democracy and the rule of law. These values, as general principles, act as a secondary source of law and they also serve to inform the other laws. For example, the principle of equality permeates the civil or criminal procedure by requiring that the procedure be accessible to all parties and that all such parties be granted equal opportunities.

## Jurisprudence

Jurisprudence consists of the decisions which are made by the Supreme Court in the sense that it interprets and applies the legal rules. It is the application and interpretation of the law, but it is not recognized within the legal system as a source of law.

## Legislative Procedure

In Spain, the general procedure for creating new laws, in theory, encourages discussion and openness, although, in practice, it is debatable whether such objectives are achieved. Legislative procedure in Spain is regulated principally by Title III, Chapter 2 of the Spanish Constitution of 1978. Under Article 87 the government may lay an initiative or proposal before the *Congreso de los Diputados*. The governmental proposal consists of a *proyecto de ley* which is similar to a government bill and is published in the Official State Bulletin. This *proyecto* is accompanied by an *exposición de motivos* which is similar to an explanatory memorandum. This will have been developed from discussions of an *anteproyecto de ley* which is similar to a white paper, although it is not necessarily generally published. This *anteproyecto* would be produced by the relevant section of the general commission of codification. The *Congreso de los Diputados* considers the text of the government's proposal, which is then published with a stated time limit for submitting amendments. Any amendments suggested are then debated. If, however, no amendments are suggested, or the text is rejected, this decision will be passed back to the general commission of codification which debates the text. Once approved by the *Congreso de los Diputados*, the text is then passed on to the senate which follows a similar procedure, and will refer any objections or amendments back to the *Congreso de los Diputados* to make a decision. In effect, the *Congreso de los Diputados* has much more influence than the senate. The text emerges from this process to receive royal assent. When the king has formally introduced the law, it is published in the Official State Bulletin, with a date fixed for its entry into force.

A legislative proposal may also be initiated through the *Congreso* and/or the *Senado* by groups of members of parliament in the form of *proposiciones de ley* presented to the House to which they belong. The Legislative Assemblies of the Autonomous Communities may also initiate legislation indirectly be asking the government to adopt a *proyecto de ley*, or directly by passing a *proposición de ley* to the *Congreso de los Diputados*. It is also possible to develop legislation by popular initiative in the form of *proposiciones de ley*, although the opportunities for this are restricted.

## References and Further Reading

De Otto, Ignacio, *Derecho Constitucional – Sistema de Fuentes* (1993, Ariel, Barcelona).
López Guerra, Luís *et al.*, *Derecho Constitucional*, vol. I, 3rd edn (1997, Tirant lo Blanch, Valencia).

Merino Merchán, José Fernando *et al.*, *Lecciones de Derecho Constitucional* (1995, Tecnos, Madrid).

Piniella Sorli, Juan-Sebastián, *Sistema de Fuentes y Bloque de Constitucionalidad – Encrucijada de Competencias* (1994, Bosch, Barcelona).

Rubio Llorente, Francisco, *La Forma del Poder – Estudios Sobre La Constitución* (1993, Centro de Estudios Constitucionales, Madrid).

# 5   Constitutional Rights

The fundamental rights of persons are covered by the Spanish Constitution. Spain is also party to a number of treaties which grant and recognize human rights. For example, Spain is party to the Universal Declaration of Human Rights, the International Agreement on Civil and Political Rights 1966 and the International Agreement on Economic, Social and Political Rights 1966 (both signed by Spain on 28 September 1976 and ratified on the 27 April 1977), the European Convention for the Protection of Human Rights and Fundamental Freedoms 1950 (signed by Spain on 24 November 1977, ratified on 26 September 1979 and entered into force by publication in the Official State Bulletin on 10 October 1979) the European Social Charter 1961 (signed by Spain on 27 April 1978 and ratified on the 29 April 1980).

The main rights and freedoms are encapsulated within the Spanish Constitution of 1978. This chapter will provide a brief survey of the rights and liberties contained in the constitution and how they are guaranteed and suspended. Before proceeding with the survey, it may be helpful to describe briefly the history of the constitutional treatment of rights in Spain.

## History of Human Rights Treatment in Spanish Law

In Spanish history the creation of human rights was seen as a way of curtailing abuse of political power. Thus, as in mediaeval England with her Magna Carta, in Spain the *Cortes de León* managed, in 1188, to persuade the King, Alfonso IX, to hold a referendum on the right of the accused to dispose of a legal process, or that of the inviolability of life, reputation, domicile and property. The institution of the *Justicia Mayor de Aragón* in the fourteenth century was also achieved in order to control the exercise of so-called 'legally constituted powers'.

The 1812 constitution of Cádiz contained a number of rights and freedoms as a consequence of the principles of liberty and equality which characterized that constitutional document. There were no such rights and liberties contained in the 1834 statute, whereas the 1837 constitution contained a separate section dedicated to a declaration of rights. These rights were reduced in the 1845 constitution. Most notably, the freedom of the press was curtailed, since the press was coming to be regarded as dangerous. The popular revolts that led to the 1869 constitution also resulted in an increase of rights within that constitution, together with provisions for the guarantee of such rights. The 1873 draft federal republican constitution, which never came to fruition, also contained many rights which were based on the rights of the person. The constitution of the restoration of 1876, although containing rights, was more restrictive, causing some of those rights to be dependent on the existence of *leyes ordinarias*, such laws themselves curtailing the rights to an extent. The 1931 constitution contained a section on the rights and duties of Spanish citizens and also distinguished between individual and political guarantees and social rights of the family, economy and culture. That constitution also laid the foundations for the so-called 'recurso de amparo', a right of appeal to the court on the basis of lack of constitutionality of a political action which might include an invasion of a constitutional right.

**Human Rights and Liberties Contained in the Spanish Constitution of 1978**

The Spanish Constitution has dedicated a broad title to the subject of fundamental rights and duties. In reality, however, not all of the rights have an identical nature, nor do they enjoy equal use and protection. There are three basic categories of rights within the constitution: fundamental rights in a strict sense, constitutional rights and principles which guide social and economic policy. Although the main section on rights appears from Article 10 to Article 55, there are other rights located in different sections of the constitution, such as voting rights, which may be found in Article 68, or the right to use Castilian, contained in Article 3. Apart from the rights actually contained in the constitution, the 1978 document also makes reference to the international treaties to which Spain is party. Furthermore, Article 10.2 states expressly that the rights and liberties contained in the constitution are to be interpreted in accordance with the Universal Declaration of Human Rights and other international treaties. It has been suggested by De Esteban and González-Trevijano (1992) that the inclusion of express rights within the constitution is a result of the history of the Spanish Constitution: rather than simply referring to the Universal Declaration and other international treaties, the creators of the constitution preferred to make use of the constitution as a means of guaranteeing such rights as well as providing limits and controls on their use.

Title I of the Constitution is structured in five separate chapters. These divide the rights into different categories. Thus Chapter 1 refers to age and nationality, characteristics which may be necessary for the enjoyment of certain specific rights. For example, the right to vote depends on the attainment of the age of majority. The second chapter is concerned generally with rights and liberties and is further divided into fundamental rights and public freedoms and the rights and duties of citizenship. The third chapter refers to the principles which guide social and economic policy. Finally, the fourth and fifth chapters make reference respectively to the guarantees and suspension of the rights and liberties contained in the constitution.

Although these categories appear to be straightforward there is, in reality, some debate about the appropriateness of some of the provisions within the sections in which they appear. For example, it could be argued that some of those rights which are contained in the chapter on rights and duties of citizens should have appeared instead in the chapter on fundamental rights such as the right to marry. Conversely, it could be argued that some of the rights which are identified as fundamental might have been more appropriately placed in the chapter relating to rights and duties of citizens. The right to work might also have been well placed in the chapter containing the principles for guiding social and economic policy.

The first chapter is concerned with the status of an individual, which includes reference to that person's age and nationality. Prior to these aspects of status, Article 10 states that the dignity of the person, the inviolable rights which are inherent in the person, the free development of personality, and respect for the law and rights are the basis of the political order and social peace. Human dignity is treated doctrinally as the point of departure for the protection of human rights in Spanish law. Dignity is recognized on a general basis, and constitutes a spiritual and moral value inherent in the person that is manifested by self-determination and conscience and responsibility for one's own life and by showing respect for others. The principle of equality is stated in Article 14 and is expressed as all Spanish people being equal before the law, without which discrimination can prevail by reason of birth, race, sex, religion, opinion or any other condition or personal or social circumstance.

Within this chapter, the specific aspects of status are those relating to age and nationality, with some consequences arising from being identified as foreign. With regard to age, Article 12 provides that Spaniards reach the age of majority at 18 years. This age is a prerequisite for the enjoyment of certain rights, such as the right to participate in political matters. However, the constitution is very general, making only a passing reference to the age of majority for civil law matters, such as the right to enter into contractual relations, and the age of majority for criminal matters is not dealt with at all by the constitution.

## Fundamental Rights in a Strict Sense

The fundamental rights contained in the constitution are provided by Article 14, which expresses the principle of equality, and in section 1 of Chapter 2 in Title I of the constitution, Articles 15–29.

### Article 15: Right to Life and Physical and Moral Integrity

This right constitutes a fundamental and pivotal right without which the other rights could not possibly exist. The recognition of this right is achieved by the prohibition of submission to torture or punishments or degrading and inhuman treatments. This is expressed by the right to physical and moral integrity through which the inviolability of the individual person is protected, and covers not only attacks aimed at injuring the person physically or spiritually but also acts to which the individual has not consented. A further recognition of this right is the abolition of the death penalty with the exception of the possibility of a death penalty in a military sense in times of war. One problem is the potential clash between this right and the right to abortion or the right to euthanasia or suicide and even sterilization.

### Article 16: Freedom of Ideology, Religion and Beliefs

With this right, no one is obliged to make a declaration about his or her ideology, religion or beliefs. Public bodies have a double obligation of respecting the beliefs of the society and maintaining with the Catholic Church and other religious orders the required relations of collaboration. The limits of this right are the protection of the rights of others to exercise their public liberties and fundamental rights and the safeguarding of security, health and public morality.

### Article 17: Individual Freedom and Security and Habeas Corpus

Nobody can be deprived of their liberty except with the observance of certain procedures and principles. A preventative detention must not last longer than is necessary for the realization of the investigations needed to establish the correct facts and, in any case, after a maximum period of 72 hours the detainee should be released or brought before the court. The detainee should be informed of his or her rights and reasons for his or her detention and cannot be obliged to speak. Every detainee has a right to the assistance of a lawyer in all police and judicial dealings. The principle of *habeas corpus* is to obtain an immediate judicial hearing for anyone detained illegally.

*Article 18: Right to Reputation, Personal and Family Privacy and to One's Own Identity*

This right covers privacy at home and in communications. One cannot make an entry or register someone in a domicile without their consent or judicial resolution, except in a case of proven criminal activity. The secrecy of all postal, telegraph and telephone communications is guaranteed except where there is judicial authorization to break such secrecy. The use of information must respect this right of privacy. It is necessary to balance this right with the right to freedom of speech and of the press.

*Article 19: Right to Freedom of Choice of Place to Live*

This right includes free movement throughout the national territory, and freedom to enter and leave Spain.

*Article 20: Freedom of Expression, Freedom of Knowledge and Right to True Information*

The freedom of expression is manifested in various forms which include the right to express and disseminate thoughts, ideas and opinions by word, in writing or any other means of publicity, and the right of literary and artistic, scientific and technical production and creation. The right is also manifested in the right of academic freedom and the right to communicate and receive accurate information. These rights may not be infringed by censure and only by judicial decision may publications, manuscripts or other means of information be seized. The right to freedom of expression may be limited by the right to reputation and personal and family privacy, as well as the protection of children and young persons.

*Article 21: Right of Assembly and to Demonstrate*

The right to peaceful meetings without arms does not require prior authority although where meetings or demonstrations are to take place in a public venue it may be necessary to inform the local authority, which may only refuse permission on grounds of danger to public order and danger to persons or property.

*Article 22: Freedom of Association*

Associations which pursue illegal objectives are prohibited, as are paramilitary and secret associations. Associations are required to be registered and they may only be dissolved or their activities suspended following a court order. Associations may take many forms, ranging from commercial partnerships or companies to public entities. Unions and industrial associations are set up in order to protect employees or employers and the conditions for their creation are simply that they comply with the constitution and the law and that they function democratically.

### Article 23: Right to Universal Suffrage and to Hold Public Office

These rights include the right to participate in public matters, including the right to vote as well as the right to be elected for public office, the right to participate in public matters through representatives freely elected in periodic elections by universal suffrage, the right to accede in conditions of equality to public office and to carry out public duties within the requirements of the law.

### Article 24: Right to Obtain Effective Protection by the Courts and Right of Access to Courts

This right is demonstrated by the right to ordinary trial predetermined by law, the right to a defence and the assistance of a lawyer and to use appropriate means of defence, the right to be informed of the charge against oneself, the right to public process without undue delays and with all safeguards, the right not to testify against oneself and not to confess guilt, and the right to a presumption of innocence, meaning that no one is guilty until proven so. Connected with this right is the principle of legality by which no one can be accused of a crime that has not been previously established and no sanctions can be imposed which have not already been established in law.

### Article 25: Right not to be Punished where there is no Crime

This Article states that where there is no legally recognized offence there should be no punishment. It also states that where an individual is sentenced to imprisonment then that punishment should be directed towards re-education and rehabilitation and should not consist of forced labour. Prisoners have a right to be paid for their work.

### Article 26: Protection of Reputation

This Article states that courts of honour are prohibited in the context of civil administration and professional organizations.

*Article 27: Right to Education and Instruction*

This right includes a right to receive an education and requires public bodies to guarantee an education to all and that parents may receive for their children an education that corresponds with their religious and moral convictions. Corresponding with this right is the rule that basic education is obligatory and free. A related right is the right to academic freedom and the freedom to establish centres of learning, as well as recognition of the autonomy of universities.

*Article 28: Right to Form Trade Unions*

This Article provides for the right to form, and be a member of, a trade union, with the possible exception of members of the armed forces and with certain limitations on those who work in the civil service. Unions also have the right to form confederations and to form, or join, international union organizations.

The Article also provides for the right to strike, although the law should provide guarantees for the maintenance of essential community services.

*Article 29: Right of Petition*

Spanish citizens have the right to petition individually and collectively in writing, while members of the armed forces may only do so individually.


The guarantees granted to these fundamental rights are that they are automatically binding and have direct effect and that all public bodies are bound to the rights and liberties recognized in Chapter 2 of Title I. In this way the fundamental rights are not just rules of action directed towards the legislator to put into effect. Rather, they have immediate effect and bind judges and courts. In this way, they are not principles for creating programmes but grant rights and obligations immediately. The essential contents of these rights are also guaranteed by the constitution. Article 53.1 states that the exercise of such rights can only be regulated by law which respects the essential contents of the rights and it is for the constitutional court to resolve conflicts over the constitutionality of such regulations and how they affect the rights. Furthermore, regulation of the use of such rights is to be reserved to an organic law according to Article 81 of the constitution.

Judicial protection of such rights is achieved by use of a preferential and summary procedure. This is provided for by Law No. 62 of 1978 on the Judicial Protection of the Fundamental Rights of the Individual. It is also possible to protect these rights by means of judicial review in the constitutional court. Finally, such rights can be used against third parties since the rights have horizontal as well as vertical effect, meaning that they can be invoked against other individuals as well as against public bodies.

## Constitutional Rights

The second category of rights comprises the constitutional rights outlined in Articles 30–38 under the heading of rights and duties of citizens. Technically, these are not fundamental rights but are mere constitutional rights. However, this category includes some very important rights such as the right to private property and to succession; the right to work; the right to collective bargaining and to adopt means of collective conflict; and freedom of enterprise within the framework of the market economy. Generally, this category of rights enjoys similar status to the fundamental rights, but they do not enjoy the preferential and summary judicial protection that the rights in the first chapter of this title enjoy.

These constitutional rights include the duty and right to defend Spain, including the right to conscientious objection and the consequent establishment of the provision of social or community service in place of military service; and the duty to maintain public spending by means of contributing to a tax system which is established according to the principles of equality and progressiveness. The chapter also provides for the right to health protection, a right of access to culture, a right to enjoy an adequate environment, a right to a dignified and adequate lifestyle, a right of young persons to participate in political, social, economic and cultural development, a right for mentally and physically disabled persons to receive treatment, rehabilitation and social integration, protection of old persons, and consumer and user protection.

Generally, constitutional rights enjoy similar status to the fundamental rights and duties above and in this way the rights in this category are binding on public bodies, have direct effect and must at least be granted to the level of their essential content. On the other hand, they do not enjoy preferential treatment in court procedures and they cannot be the subject of the *recurso de amparo* before the constitutional court. The rights which fall within this category are varied in style and content. For example, the right to property does not enjoy judicial preference, but the positive law pays considerable attention to this right. On the other hand, the right to work is dependent on another subject, the employer, to provide such work.

Article 38 of the constitution also contains a right of enterprise within the framework of the market economy. The freedom of enterprise is regarded as a fundamental element of the constitution. However, it is not an unlimited right and, indeed, has to be balanced against the principle set out in Article 128, which states that all wealth in whatever form is a matter of public interest and that economic initiative lies with the public sector reserving, in particular to public bodies, essential services and monopolies and allowing the participation of private enterprises where the public interest allows it. Another way in which the right is restricted is that it must form part of a general system so that, for example, it will not be possible to keep a shop open at all hours because other rights and conditions such as working hours should be respected. The state's role focuses on protecting the functioning of the market which is a necessary condition for the enjoyment of the right of freedom of enterprise. This provides a role for consumer protection law and for competition law which protects the freedom of enterprise from a more utilitarian perspective.

## The Guiding Principles of Social and Economic Policy

The third chapter in the first title sets out the guiding principles of social and economic policy. These lack the qualities of the rights set out in the second chapter since they are not directly legally binding. They do not impose an objective limit on the legislator with a minimum content and their effectiveness depends on the actions of the legislator. Effectively, they require further legislation in order to have any practical effect. Then their effectiveness depends on the extent to which the legislation follows their direction. They tend to be rhetorical in nature and cover a wide range of ideals to be pursued by the political, legal and economic system. For example, they include statements of upholding the principles of the family, such as that parents should support their children within or outside marriage until they reach the age of majority; that public bodies should promote and protect culture and should promote scientific advances and research for the benefit of all; that all Spaniards should have the right to enjoy a dignified and adequate lifestyle; that public authorities should guarantee consumer protection by effective procedures so that their health and safety and legitimate economic interests are covered; and that the old should be protected.

It is important to remember that the constitution sets out duties as well as rights for its citizens and, from this perspective, it is worth highlighting these duties. A number of the duties have corresponding rights. Thus, for example, there is the duty to know Castilian Spanish contained in Article 13, since Castilian is the official Spanish language. This duty corresponds with the right to be able to use Castilian. Similarly, Article 30 provides both a right and a duty in national security: all citizens may enjoy security and they must respect this as a national need. The duty to work, in Article 35, corresponds with a right to work, to free choice of profession or office, to promotion through work and to a wage sufficient to satisfy the needs of the worker and his or her family. While there are duties which are related to rights, the constitution also contains some duties which stand independently: for example, the duty to pay taxes or the duty of parents to support their children who are still within the age of minority.

## Guarantees of Fundamental Rights and Freedoms

The principle of institutional guarantee of fundamental rights comes from German law and is based on the reality that the theoretical recognition of human rights in a constitution is not sufficient for the realization and enjoyment of those rights. Such rights require to be given effect as well as being stated in a written document. As a result of this realist position, the constitution establishes a complex system for the protection and effectiveness of the rights which are recognized within that constitution. This principle is reinforced by the structural mechanism of institutional guarantees of such rights, the view being that such rights would have little value if they were not constitutionally guaranteed. In this way, for example, the law indirectly protects the constitutional rights by making difficult their elaboration or modification. Thus, for example, the constitution demands that laws which concern or affect the fundamental rights must take the form of organic laws. In this way delegated legislation will not be allowed to regulate rights or duties of citizens which appear in Title I of the constitution. The forms of guarantee are fourfold: first, the rights are binding on public authorities; secondly, there are positive legislative rules which make certain actions which turn these rights into effect mandatory; thirdly, they may be protected in the courts; and fourthly, they may be protected by the *Defensor del Pueblo*, whose position is like that of an ombudsman.

The binding nature of the rights on public bodies is a conceptual safeguard against derecognition or disregard of such rights by those bodies which have competence to create their own rules. Thus their rules or regulations must at least be consistent with the recognition of rights contained in the constitution. On another level it is possible for citizens whose rights might have been infringed to implement procedures for preventing or stopping an infringement or obstruction of their rights by public bodies. In this way the protection of rights from challenge by public bodies operates on two levels: one as a general abstract level which acts as a prevention, the other level being a reactive mechanism by which it is possible to defend actively an attempt to interfere with or infringe upon the rights provided by the constitution. At the first level, protection is offered by the fact that certain of the rights are directly applicable, not requiring implementing laws for their effectiveness. Thus Article 53.1 states that the rights in Chapter 2 of the Constitution are binding on all public bodies. This principle has been reinforced by other legislation. For example, the *Ley Orgánica 6/85 del Poder Judicial* states in Article 7 that the fundamental rights and public freedoms bind in their entirety all judges and courts and are guaranteed protection by those judges and courts. This direct applicability of the rights and liberties has the effect of preventing negative legislation.

Legal rules to protect the rights recognized in the constitution may be used to regulate the exercise of the fundamental rights. For example, the reserve of the *ley orgánica* has the effect of preventing some bodies from creating contrary regulations. In this way *decretos leyes* – emergency legislation – may not, under Article 86, affect the fundamental rights and liberties contained in the constitution. Furthermore, the fact that the rights may only be regulated by a formal law means that a majority of the congress is necessary for such a law to be introduced. This itself acts as a safeguard of the constitutional rights. In reality, the *ley orgánica* sets the conditions for the exercise of rights provided by the constitution, but these are then further developed by *leyes ordinaries*. It is not possible for lower-level legislation to avoid affecting in some way the rights provided by the constitution. Conversely, the *ley orgánica* is reserved for certain aspects of the constitution and is not to be used in every situation: otherwise, the importance of the *ley orgánica* would be undermined. Furthermore, it is necessary for the *ley orgánica* to be produced with respect to the essential contents of the constitutional right.

Protection of constitutional rights and freedoms by the courts and judiciary occurs in a variety of ways. These constitute the reactive ways in which an individual can seek to protect those rights which they consider to have been infringed. It is possible to use both the ordinary courts and the constitutional court. Therefore, as well as using the ordinary court procedures, it is possible to use the constitutional court by the procedure known as *recurso de amparo constitucional*. The judicial protection available is regulated first by the *Ley 62/78 de Protección Jurisdiccional de los Derechos Fundamentales de la Persona*. However, this law was approved before the constitution was finalized and so does not make reference to the constitutional rights. Therefore a number of other specific laws provide court procedures by which specific rights may be protected, such as the *Ley Orgánica 6/84 Reguladora del Habeas Corpus* (Regulatory Organic Law on *Habeus Corpus*), and the *Ley Orgánica 1/82 de Protección del Derecho al Honor, a la Intimidad Personal y Familiar y a la Propia Imagen* (Organic Law on the Protection of the Right to Preserve One's Reputation, the Right to Personal and Family Privacy and to One's Identity), as well as the *Decreto Legislativo 2/95 de Procedimiento Laboral* (Legislative Decree on Labour Law Procedure). All of these specific laws offer procedures through the ordinary courts. An additional procedure is provided in Article 53.2 which is limited exclusively to the rights provided in Articles 14 to 29. This is different from the ordinary court procedures. It is also notable that this special procedure is designed to be speedier than the other ordinary court procedures as well as offering priority over actions which follow the ordinary procedures. One consequence of these two characteristics is that the special procedure has shorter time limits and is less complex.

The role of the *Defensor del Pueblo* is envisaged in Article 54 of the constitution which provides that a *ley orgánica* shall regulate that institution as a high parliamentary commissioner whose role is to defend the rights provided in Title I of the constitution, with the task of supervising the activities of the state administration and giving account to the *Cortes Generales*. The institution of the *Defensor del Pueblo* is regulated by the *Ley Orgánica 3/81 del 6 de abril del Defensor del Pueblo*. The role of the *Defensor del Pueblo* is like that of the Ombudsman in the UK, to supervise the activity of the administration in order to detect possible violations of the rights recognized in the constitution and to instigate the rectification of such conduct. In this way the *Defensor del Pueblo* does not have executive powers but only powers of persuasion and can act directly as well as by means of reports to the parliament. Thus the role of the *Defensor del Pueblo* is more political than one carrying legal weight.

The *Defensor del Pueblo* is appointed for five years with a renewable tenure. The qualifications required are that he or she is Spanish and of the age of majority and is able to enjoy all civil and political rights. He or she is given full independent status and also enjoys parliamentary privilege and immunity. It is also possible for the *Defensor del Pueblo* to delegate his or her tasks to a deputy. The ambit of competence of the *Defensor del Pueblo* covers every authority, functionary or person who acts within the public administration and the actions of the *Defensor del Pueblo* may be initiated by the *Defensor del Pueblo* or at the initiative of a natural or legal person with a legitimate interest. His or her services are provided free. He or she has powers of inspection and investigation and the public bodies are obliged to cooperate with those investigations. The *Defensor del Pueblo* may provide a report in which he or she establishes whether the functionary or public body has provoked the complaint through abuse, arbitrariness, discrimination, error negligence or omission. The *Defensor del Pueblo* may also make suggestions for improvement and may also make the decision known to the state fiscal general. It is also possible for the *Defensor del Pueblo* to instigate court procedures of claims of unconstitutionality or the *recurso de amparo*. Similar figures exist at the level of the autonomous communities.

## References and Further Reading

Calvo Meijide, Alberto, *Introducción al Derecho Publico y Privado* (1994, Prensa y Ediciones Iberoamericanos, Madrid).

De Esteban, Jorge and González-Trevijano, Pedro J., *Curso de Derecho Constitucional Español I* (1992, Civitas, Madrid).

López Guerra, Luís *et al.*, *Derecho Constitucional*, vol. I, 3rd edn (1997, Tirant lo Blanch, Valencia).

Martín-Retortillo, Luís and De Otto, Ignacio, *Derechos Fundamentales y Constitución* (1988, Centro de Estudios Constitucionales, Madrid).

Olivan López, Ezquierra Serrano and Muñoz, Blasquez, *Introducción al Derecho*, 3rd edn (1993, Tecnos, Madrid).

Peces-Barba Martínez, G., *Curso de Derechos Fundamentales* (1991, Centro de Estudios Constitucionales, Madrid).

# 6 Public Administration and Administrative Law

The public administration in Spain is a complex organization which has undergone important changes as Spain's society and political system have been transformed and developed. For example, the transition from an autocratic state to a democracy has created a new character for the administrative organization, as has the transition from a unitary state to a state made up of autonomous communities. From this point of view, the administration is made up of various sections ranging from the government, which has a national role, to the organizations of the autonomous communities, to local entities such as the provincial deputies, and municipalities as well as independent organizations. Thus the expression 'public administration' does not simply mean one organization but a whole coordinated network of different bodies and organizations. Another notable characteristic is the growth in importance of the administration as the interventionism of the state increases. This has also led to a need to modernize the administration periodically. A number of important laws were created during the 1960s which affected the structure, procedures and human resources of the administration.

The transition towards democracy had the effect of putting administration onto a second plane. This was seen as necessary since the administration had become static under Franco's rule. Further, the establishment of the autonomous communities led to the principle of decentralization, although the model of each such community administration is very similar, providing almost a uniformity of structures.

Morell Ocaña (1996) defines public administration as the institution in which are integrated those public law entities with a special legal quality. Such entities have the role of managing the aims of the public interest under full submission to the law and legislation. The public administration is a part of the state establishment. It is shaped by the rules laid out in the constitution. In particular, Articles 1, 2 and 137 are especially relevant. Article 1 states that sovereignty resides in the Spanish people and Article 2 recognizes the right to autonomy of the nationalities and regions which make up the Spanish nation. Article 137 makes clear that the state is made up of territorial collective groups. Following these articles, the Law of Public Administration recognizes the following administrative bodies: the general state administration, the administrations of the autonomous communities and the entities which make up the local administration. Article 2(2) of the Law of Public Administration also makes clear that the administrative bodies are subject to the law.

The Spanish Constitution provides, in Article 103:

(1) The public administration aims to serve the public interest and acts according to the principles of efficacy, hierarchy, decentralization, deconcentration and coordination, and with respect for the law.
(2) The organs of the State Administration are created, directed and coordinated in accordance with the law.
(3) The law shall regulate the status of public servants, access to the civil service in accordance with the principles of merit, capability, the peculiarities of the exercise of the right to associate, the system of incompatibilities and guarantees of impartiality in the exercise of their functions.

Articles 103–7 set out the principles for the organization and activities of the public administration. The social and democratic state requires a complex and developed administration in order to carry out the functions with which it is charged. For example, Article 9.2 of the constitution requires the public bodies to promote the conditions for freedom and equality of individuals and groups and to remove the obstacles that prevent their fulfilment, as well as to facilitate the participation of citizens in political, economic, social and cultural life.

## The Structure of the Administration

There are various pillars of administration ranging from the administration of the state to the administration of the autonomous communities, the local entities, and other entities which have an institutional or corporative nature. The complexity of the structure of the state means that there exist a variety of different public administrations. For example, there exists both a state-level public administration and a regional or territorial level public administration. Some powers are reserved in the constitution for a central administrative body. At the same time, each of the autonomous communities is organized with an administrative body in order to carry out its respective powers. The constitution also recognizes the autonomy for carrying out their interests of certain other regional entities which have their own administrations. A further peripheral administration exists for the state to be able to operate with a territorial structure. According to Morell Ocaña, the territorial entities are organized in such a way that they can comply collectively with their two essential functions: representation and administration. They do this by each having a territorial parliament which has the representative function, and a territorial government which administers the decisions, of the parliament. The local administrations do not have their functions split in this way and the same local town halls carry out both representative and administrative functions.

Besides the territorially based administrations there exist other administrative bodies which are separated from the territorial framework but which are bound in one way or another to the territorial administrations. There are two main groups of non-territorial administrations which have a corporate or institutional base. These are public corporations which have a personal element, such as the *Colegios Profesionales*, and public bodies such as those with a specified public objective with an administrative role, such as the national health institute or the post office – the *correos y telegrafos*. Although these bodies have their own legal personality and identity, they each rely on local-level administration. These bodies vary considerably in the tasks that they must carry out and some of them such as the Bank of Spain, enjoy a significant level of autonomy.

Other administrative bodies have no territorial connection, nor are they bound to the state administration. For example, certain bodies which carry out state activities, such as the *Cortes Generales* and the *Tribunal Constitutional*, have their own administrative structures. These bodies each have their own administrative organs for carrying out their functions. Another example is the ombudsman, the *Defensor del Pueblo*. Other examples include public service television and nuclear defence. These are regarded as neutral or independent. In these neutral bodies there is a guaranteed presence of political or cultural minorities.

Cazorla Prieto and Arnaldo Alcubilla (1988) suggest that administrative law has developed in such a way as to emphasize the importance of the rules of organization as a result of the state's political development from being a laissez-faire state, to an interventionist state, to a planning state. Within the rule of law the administrative body must not impose itself on society, but serve society instead.

## The Nature of the Administrative Organization

According to García Trevijano (1957), administrative law is not a law of administrative organization but, on the contrary, the organization gains legal status when there exists an administrative law. The legal status of the organization arises from the fact that each of the organs which make up the administration have defined powers which serve as a counterweight for them against the other organs.

## The Legal Base

The rules of organization have become increasingly more important and this has been reinforced by the constitution. Additionally, codification of the rules of administrative law continues to develop. The main formal laws are the *Ley de Régimen de la Administración del Estado de 1956* and the *Ley de Procedimiento Administrativo de 1958*. The law relating to local administrative activities is the *Ley de Bases de Régimen Local* and of further relevance is the *Ley de Entidades Estatales Autónomas*. A third level of rules is of those regulations and provisions created by the executive body of the administration. A number of characteristics mark the organization of the administration: uniformity and unity, independence from the government, and subordination to the higher state organs such as the parliament. The dynamic nature of the administration means that it is subject to change. This is necessary as a result of the changing nature of the state, from an interventionist state to a state planning system.

## Constitutional Principles of Administration

The principles of administration set out in the constitution were influenced by the French Revolution and have been modified by the modern idea of the social state. These principles include the submission of the administration to the legal system; the state structure; organization and structure of the public administrations, including the principles of decentralization and deconcentration, the principle of coordination and the principle of organic legality; principles relative to administrative action, including objectivity, efficacy, participation of the citizen and responsibility of the administration; and the regime of civil servants.

As has been noted above, Article 103 of the constitution states that the public administration will comply with the law and this suggests that the administration must respect the principle of the rule of law. It also means that the administration is subject to the whole system and hierarchy of legal sources. This is because the administrative body is part of the executive which implements the decisions of the parliament, which enjoys the supreme position in this hierarchy since it exercises the sovereignty of the people by parliamentary representation of their views. Further, even where the administration is granted discretionary powers, these must not be applied without obedience to the law. Finally, submission to the law implies that the administration must be granted prior powers before acting. It must also be noted that because the administration is subject to the law this means that its actions are controlled by the courts and judges. The administration develops the objectives of the laws and the rest of the legal system.

As regards the territorial aspect of the administration, it is clear that, under Article 149.1.18 of the constitution, the central powers will set out the basic framework of the legal regime of the different administrations, of the civil servants, and the rules of their activities. This framework can be found in the Law of 26 November 1992, number 30, called Legal Regime of Public Administrations and the Common Administrative Procedure.

The other principles set out in Article 103 apply generally not only at state level but also at the territorial level. The principle of hierarchy reflects the pyramidal hierarchical structure of the administration. The government is at the top of the hierarchy, followed by a number of sectorial ministries which have their own multiple subdivisions. One aspect of the principle of hierarchy is that it makes possible the unity between the different administrative organs. The hierarchy is both linear and functional. In practice, the principle of hierarchy means that those organs in the higher sphere may direct and instruct those in the lower sphere as well as supervise their activities. This is recognized in the *Ley de Régimen de la Administración del Estado*. The government directs the administration in the way it carries out the administration.

The principle of competence is basically concerned with the division of labour between the different organs and is aimed at achieving an efficient organization. The principle of decentralization is, in part, implicit in the decentralized structure of the state of autonomous communities and it may also be understood as a principle which enables the creation of special administrations for the provision of specified services. This consists in the handing over of functions from one administrative entity to other administrative entities at a lower level. This can be at a territorial or institutional level. The principle of deconcentration is linked to that of decentralization and refers to the need to base decisions on and carry out administrative functions relative to the needs of individual citizens. This process can be vertical, between a superior central organ and another, inferior, central organ or horizontal, between a central organ and a peripheral organ. The principle of coordination goes beyond having a hierarchical stucture and requires that the relations between the different administrations and aspects of administration are linked rationally and effectively. For example, Article 98 of the constitution states that the president directs the activity of the government and coordinates the functions of the other members without prejudice to their competence and responsibilities. The principle of organic legality requires that the organs of the administration be created in a democratic manner and by the parliament and developed from rules created by the government.

The actions of the administration must be carried out according to certain principles. The principle of objectivity or neutrality and the principle of impartiality are set out in Article 103 of the constitution. The principle of objectivity in a democratic state requires that the administration acts on the instructions of the government. Additionally, it requires that the administration submit itself to the rule of law, in order to guarantee to the citizen freedom from arbitrary decisions. Thus the combination of the administration being required to carry out policies of the government and at the same time being subject to the rule of law protects the individual. The principle of efficacy requires the administration to act efficiently and in such a way that the citizen can benefit. However, this does not allow the administration to act outside established procedures and legal requirements. The principle of citizen participation is an aspect of the democratic objective of the constitution. This principle is elaborated upon in Article 105, in which it is stated that the citizen has a right to be heard in the creation of the rules which will affect him or her, in access to registers and archives, or in the right to be heard in an administrative procedure. A general aspect of this right is that the administration has a duty to provide citizens with information. The principle of responsibility of the administration is found in Article 106 of the constitution. This principle is also a consequence of the submission of the administration to the rule of law. The principle means that the administration must indemnify individuals for harm suffered as a result of administrative action. Furthermore, civil servants may find themselves personally liable for wrongs.

Civil servants are also subject to a particular set of rules. In the first place, individuals must meet certain conditions for access to the civil service based on merit and capacity. The second rule is that civil servants may form a union, but special rules apply. Thirdly, civil servants are required to be impartial in the exercise of their activities. This rule corresponds with the requirement of objectivity in administrative action. Finally, the rules which govern the activities of the civil servants must be established by means of a law in order to guarantee their legality.

## Control of the Administration

The public administration is subject to controls of a different nature – both political and legal. The political control is granted to the *Cortes Generales* since these also control the actions of the government and therefore this control extends to the administration which implements the policies of the government. The means of control open to the *Cortes* is to hold investigation commissions similar to public inquiries, although these are very rare. Another political form of control is through the *Defensor del Pueblo* by means of investigations, complaints and reports, but these have also lost their rigour.

Legal control is established by the submission to the legal system as well as to the rule of law and applies both to the organization and to the activities of the administration. There are judicial controls which are exercised by the courts and judges as well as non-judicial controls carried out by other bodies.

## Judicial Controls

Article 106.1 provides that the courts control the regulatory powers and the legality of the activities of the administration. One such form of judicial control lies in the procedure of the *contencioso-administrativo* conducted by specialized organs from within the *Poder Judicial*. However, before going to the courts, there are internal procedures which must first be exhausted. All acts of the administration are susceptible to control by their submission to the legal system, although the law itself cannot predetermine all the elements of the administrative activity, and there is a certain degree of discretion necessary for efficacy which can only be challenged where there has clearly been an abuse of this power.

The constitutional court also has powers of control over certain of the activities of the public administration. Normally, this control is subsidiary to the controls of the ordinary courts which act as a first post on the route to resolving an administrative law dispute. However, on occasion, it is posssible to go directly to the constitutional court, as with matters concerning the sharing of competences between the state and the autonomous communities and in the control of the constitutionality of acts of the autonomous communities at the instigation of the government.

As indicated above, the administrative process is known as the *recurso contencioso-administrativo*. The object of this process is to ascertain the intentions behind an administrative act. The *Ley Orgánica del Poder Judicial de 1985* did envisage in Articles 90 and 91 new organs of first instance, the *Juzgados de lo Contencioso-Administrativo*, which have still not been established. Consequently, the jurisdiction of this process follows the *Ley de la Jurisdicción Contencioso-Administrativo de 1956* (Procedural Law of Administrative Dispute Resolution) which granted jurisdiction to the *Salas*

*de lo Contencioso-Administrativo de los Tribunales Superiores de Justicia* –
the administrative law branches of the superior courts of justice – the
*Audiencia Nacional* and the *Sala de lo Contencioso-Administrativo del
Tribunal Supremo*. These special branches of the court have jurisdiction to
hear complaints against provisions and acts of the executive and legislative
organs of an autonomous community and against the acts of the state administration. The *Sala de lo Contencioso-Administrativo del Tribunal Supremo* is regarded as an organ of first instance as well as appeal hearings. It
is also the court which has competence for judging complaints against the
acts and provisions of the council of ministers or their delegated commissions, acts of the *Consejo General del Poder Judicial*, of the government
organs, of the legislative chambers, of the constitutional court, of the court
of auditors and of the *Defensor del Pueblo*.

This *recurso contencioso-administrativo* procedure may be used by public
bodies or individuals and against administrative acts as much as against
regulations (*reglamentos*) and other legal provisions of a lower level.
Through this procedure such acts or provisions may be annulled or challenged. The procedure may also be used to impose on the administration
the recognition of a particular individual legal situation or a right such as
to the grant of a licence. The court's decision will be either declaratory,
such as declaring null a provision, or an order to the administration to do
something.

There are some special procedures which apply to certain activities of the
public administration. In particular, these are concerned with the protection
of fundamental rights. For example, such procedures may include the procedure for *habeas corpus* for protecting the liberty of the individual, and the
procedure of the *recurso de amparo* for the protection of fundamental rights.

## Other Controls

Non-judicial controls include procedures for protecting fundamental rights
both generally and in relation to specific rights. For example, the *Defensor
del Pueblo* has the function of defending the rights set out in the first title of
the constitution. Another example is the Data Protection Agency, which
protects citizens as regards the use of computerized personal data.

There are also self-regulatory mechanisms in place such as those for
accounts and finance, although these seem to be merely formal rather than
judgmental controls.

## The Sources of Administrative Law

The sources of administrative law in Spain are an important aspect of the formation of the legal system generally and three matters are of particular concern in the administrative sphere: who should create the rules, about what administrative rules can be created and the form that such rules might take. These questions are relevant to the principle of hierarchy of legal rules according to what form they take and who creates them and the principle of competence which means that certain bodies only have power over certain matters.

The sharing of rule-making powers between the state and the autonomous communities is based on the legislative levels and depends on whether they are basic or developmental laws under consideration. The state is given the power to make basic legislation under Article 149 of the constitution. Basic legislation sets out the aims and objectives and general policies and is legislation which applies uniformly and throughout the whole nation and thus provides a common denominator for the rules created by all the autonomous communities, each of which may develop its own rules to suit the interests of that community. The effect of the basic legislation is to limit the extent to which the autonomous communities can create their own rules and the nature of those rules will thus be shaped by the framework provided by the basic legislation.

Developmental legislation has two different meanings. In some cases the autonomous statutes have drawn a line of exemption treating as exclusive to each community the relevent powers within those statutes. In this way, the laws of the autonomous communities only become bound to the state law in a negative way, in the sense that they should not contradict a superior or basic law. Effectively, this is not a classical hierarchy but a coordination of two separate legal systems or laws. The state law, in the areas where the autonomous communities have exclusive competences, becomes a superfluous law, but where an autonomous community has exclusive powers the state law is not considered as a basic law since the basic laws are never secondary and always have direct application. Another aspect of the developmental laws is that in which the communities create laws which are developmental rules within the framework of the legislation created at state level. In this situation there exists the classic hierarchy by which the autonomous community shall only have discretion if this is provided by the state law. Furthermore, the state law can itself be applied in each autonomous community where the community itself has not legislated on a particular subject.

Another source of law is that which is delegated to the autonomous communities by the state through a *ley ordinaria*. The state may delegate powers to the autonomous community which strictly remain within the competence of the state. At the same time the state keeps control of the delegated power by not abdicating the power but instead by simply delegating it to the autonomous community with conditions and instructions.

It is also possible for rules to be created by other entities at a local level, in particular where they create rules for their own organization. An example is provided by the rules of the local town halls which may govern the freedoms and rights of individuals within the locality. Other entities similarly creating their own rules are those such as corporations and associations that may have rules for their own administration to which they and their members will be bound.

## Personnel of the Administration

The public administration accounts for approximately 2 million employees – around 17 per cent of the workforce. The formal route to public service employment is through state exams known as *oposiciones*. These are regarded as very competitive and difficult. However, a large proportion of administrative employees do not enter public service by this route. Generally, the salaries of employees in the administrative sphere are lower than the salaries of their private sector colleagues.

## References and Further Reading

Cazorla Prieto, Luís and Arnaldo Alcubilla, Enrique, *Temas de Derecho Constitucional y Derecho Administrativo* (1988, Marcial Pons, Madrid).

Clavero Arevalo, Manuel, *Estudios de Derecho Administrativo* (1992, Civitas, Madrid).

García de Enterría, Eduardo and Rodriguez, Fernández, *Curso de Derecho Administrativo* (1997, Civitas, Madrid).

García de Enterría, Eduardo and Escalante, José, *Legislación Administrativa*, 4th edn (1996, Civitas, Madrid).

García de Enterría, Eduardo, *La Administración Española*, 4th edn (1985, Alianza, Madrid).

García-Trenjano, J.A., *Principios Jurídicos de la Organización Administrativa* (1957, Instituto Estudios Políticos, Madrid).

María Cazorla Prieto, Luís and Arnaldo Alcubilla, Enrique, *Temas de Derecho Constitucional y Derecho Administrativo* (1988, Marcial Pons, Madrid).

Morell Ocaña, Luis, *Curso de Derecho Administrativo* (1996, Aranzadi, Madrid).

Nieto García, Alejandro and Gutíerrez Reñon, Alberto, 'La Administracíon Pública', in Francisco J. Bobillo (ed.), *España a Debate – La Política* (1991, Tecnos, Madrid), 133–48.

# 7    The Autonomous Communities

One of the most important aspects of the Spanish Constitution is the territorial or regional organization of the state. Attempts to decentralize the state legal and political structure have been made since the middle of the nineteenth century. However, Spain has a history of a unitary and centralized nation state since the arrival of the Bourbons around the beginning of the eighteenth century, resulting in a tendency towards a regional unitary state with a structure based on a redistribution of the political power in the centre and the periphery. Prior to the civil war of 1936–9 there were only three regions which had developed towards autonomy: Cataluña in 1932, the Basque Country in 1936 and Galicia to a lesser degree. Franco's rule involved the creation of a unified imperial state and ended efforts to establish autonomy for a number of regions in Spain. Thus the negotiations for the 1978 constitution focused to a great extent on the question of centralism versus regionalism. The transition to democracy entailed the construction of a 'state of regions'.

This principle of a state of regions is enshrined in Article 2 of the constitution, which states:

> The Constitution is based on the complete unity of the Spanish Nation, the common and indivisible country of all Spanish people; it recognizes and guarantees the right to self-government of the nationalities and the regions of which it is composed and solidarity amongst them all.

Article 2 seeks a balance between the strong identity of the national and regional areas and the unity of the Spanish state. It is like a form of federalism characterized more by interdependence, concurrence or cooperation than by independence. The new territorial organization created by the 1978 constitution in reality is framed by a process of rationalization of political life and by a deepening of democracy, with participation of citizens and pluralism. Since 1978, Spain has created 17 autonomous communities

81

(Andalucia, Aragón, Asturias, Balearic Islands, Canary Islands, Cantabria, Castilla-la-Mancha, Castilla-León, Cataluña, Estremadura, Galicia, Madrid, Murcia, Navarra, Pais Vasco, La Rioja, Comunidad de Valencia) and two autonomous cities (Ceuta and Melilla).

Alonso Zaldívar and Castells (1993) state that the approach of the framers of the constitution to the treatment of autonomies had three dimensions:

a) At the heart of the Spanish State, the political construction of a mutually binding unity agreed by all nationalities and regions, given concrete form in each Community's Statute of Self-Government and in common respect for the Constitution and the laws and institutions derived from it.
b) Efforts to correct social and economic inequalities between regions by policies to remove imbalances and based on the regional policy of the European Community.
c) Administrative reform by transferring powers and resources to autonomies and municipalities, through a complex process of negotiation and institutional adjustments.

The constitution reflects a compromise between left-wing forces which sought to establish a federalist state structure and those on the right who wanted to retain a centralist state. The compromise has been criticized consistently for its flexibility, which gives rise to confusion and uncertainty. For example, the constitution does not define autonomy and does not state exactly which powers accompany autonomy.

The main provisions relating to autonomy are contained in Title VIII of the constitution. Article 137 of the constitution sets out the principle for the way in which the state's territory will be organized: 'The state is organized territorially in municipalities, in provinces and in the Autonomous Communities which together constitute the State. All these entities enjoy autonomy for the management of their respective interests.' The constitution shows that the Spanish nation is made up of a plurality of nationalities and regions which are an expression of the principles of cultural, historical and linguistic homogeneity of the peoples that fall into those groups. The autonomy of these entities provided for by Article 137 is qualitatively distinct; the autonomous communities enjoy a superior autonomy to the administrations of the local entities since they are also given legislative and governmental powers. In reality, they have autonomy in the management of their respective interests and this autonomy is given on the basis of national unity by which the central state must protect general public interests.

In short, since the creation of the constitution, Spain has become a state in which there are two separate and coexisting legal systems, one of the territories and the other of the state, with the constitution having a third-level role outside these two legal systems. The constitution is seen as the common link between the two systems.

## The Four Levels of State Organization

The Spanish state is organized on four levels: central state level, autonomous community level, provincial level and municipal level. The central state has a range of reserved powers which are set out in the constitution. The autonomous communities are public entities defined by a geographical collective of provinces and municipalities. They are territorial entities constituted by provinces which are linked by their historic, cultural and economic characteristics. Each autonomous community is granted legislative autonomy and capacity for self-government. In a sense, an autonomous community might be described as a mini-state, but one which is not completely independent of the central state's control. Indeed, the state reserves for itself important functions of control: in the process of assumption of powers by an autonomous community there are numerous safeguards which make room for a certain level of state intervention. On the other hand, the autonomous communities do not intervene in the running of the state by the central government.

The province is a local entity which has its own legal personality determined by the grouping of municipalities and by the necessity to comply with state activities. The powers of the province may be modified or limited by the parliament by means of a *ley orgánica*. Municipalities have a certain amount of autonomy which is guaranteed by attributing to them legal personality and granting them their own government and administration. The *Concejales* (councils) are elected by the citizens of the municipality by universal, secret, equal, free and direct suffrage. Mayors are elected by the councillors or by the citizens. The autonomous communites have a greater level of autonomy than the provinces or municipalities since they are granted political as well as administrative and legislative autonomy.

The constitution does not state the necessary criteria for creating autonomous communities, apart from requiring territories to be linked historically, culturally and economically, or that they be insular territories or isolated provinces. Article 143.1 provides that

> Exercising the right to autonomy recognized in Article 2 of the Constitution, adjoining provinces with common historical, cultural and economic characteristics, islands and provinces with an historical regional identity may accede to self-government and form autonomous communities in accordance with the provisions of this section of the Constitution and their respective statutes.

In theory, territories could have remained without autonomy status. However, although the constitution does not demand that all territories become autonomous communities, the reality is that all Spanish territories have become part of an autonomous community.


## The Concept of Autonomy

Within the Spanish constitutional context autonomy has come to be defined as the power of a territory to create its own law and legal system. This law is not only recognized by the state but is also incorporated into the state's overall legal system and is declared as legally binding on the people within that territorial region. In this way autonomy consists of the power to create legal rules both of which are integrated into the state's law and legal system and apply in a sphere of their own, exempt from specific or concrete instructions.

However, there are a number of limits to this autonomy. Thus the constitutional court, in a decision of 2 February 1981, said that autonomy refers to a limited power. Effectively, autonomy is not the same as sovereignty and, given that each territorial organization granted autonomy is part of a whole state, the principle of autonomy cannot operate as a challenge to unity since this unity is the basis upon which the autonomy is granted, as expressed by Article 2 of the constitution. This basis of unity prevents a division of Spain into separated areas. Article 137 of the constitution requires that each entity be given its own exclusive powers necessary to satisfy its own interests. At the same time, the state remains in a superior position. Furthermore, the constitutional court declared in 1981 that the right to autonomy of the nationalities and regions, which is a corollary to their solidarity, is granted with an underlying basis of national unity.

The breadth of autonomy of the autonomous communities is fixed by the state within the framework established in the constitution. Where competence over a particular issue is not adopted within the statute of autonomy, this competence remains with the state, whose rules shall prevail in any case of conflict.

Within the constitution, the structural model of the state is flexible and open and is different from the models of federal or regional states. For example, the constitution does not declare how many autonomous communities should exist; nor does the constitution prescribe an equal share of powers for the different communities; nor were all the autonomous communities to be established simultaneously. Furthermore, the constitution does not state what powers will be attributed to the different communities as is normal in federal or regional state constitutions. Despite these omissions in the constitution, the autonomous communities enjoy powers which might be the envy of many of the federal states.

## Character of the Autonomy Process

Recognition of the right to autonomy and the autonomy process contains a number of principles which may fall into the two categories of political and legal autonomy. First, the principle of generality recognizes the common historic, cultural and economic characteristics of parts of a wide territory as well as insular territories and provinces with a regional historic entity. Secondly, the principle of voluntariness means that autonomy is a potential right rather than something to be imposed on a given territory. Thirdly, the principle of graduality signifies that the establishment of autonomy is an open process and not subject to time limits. Fourthly, the process is progressive in that it leads to an increased level of integration. Fifthly, Article 148.2 of the constitution provides the possibility of increasingly wide powers, so that a territory may pass from a limited to a full autonomy. Sixthly, the principle of diversity of planning means that each autonomy can adapt its structure and functioning to its own needs. As well as the principles which surround the process of autonomy, a number of principles also guide the character of autonomy itself.

## Principles of a Constitutional Regime

A number of principles provide a framework for the organization and accommodation of autonomous communities. These principles include constitutionality, unity, autonomy, sovereignty, equality, solidarity, equilibrium, financial sufficiency, prohibition of federation of the autonomous communities, and cooperation.

The principle of *constitutionality* is regarded as axiomatic and is given primacy in Article 9.1 of the constitution, declaring the superior value of the constitution as a legal norm which is directly applicable to all public bodies. Autonomy is in one sense dialectically opposed to the principle of *unity* and has two dimensions, autonomy as a law and autonomy as a form of organization and functioning of the state, and is manifested by giving to local public entities powers and competences. *Autonomy* itself does not count as sovereignty, but is a political autonomy with regard to the administration of the provinces and municipalities. In this sense it is a form of political self-government.

The principle of *equality* allows each autonomous community equality as to what goes into the contents of the constitutional framework. There is not a single formula, but a framework of competences which are offered by the constitution. Although the different constitutions and competences of the different communities may not be the same, that does not allow certain communities economic or social privileges over the others. All citizens are granted equality regardless of what community they reside in. They all have the same rights and obligations in every part of the Spanish territory. Article 139.2 also grants to them freedom of movement and the state has the ultimate responsibility for guaranteeing equality among people. In this way the autonomous communities cannot themselves legislate over these matters.

The principle of *solidarity* is included in Article 2 of the constitution and this solidarity applies between the nationalities and regions and the state and between the nationalities and regions themselves. In this way the communities participate in the state's activities through the senate as the chamber of territorial representation for legislative initiatives and so on. In addition, such solidarity limits the actions of the communities so that they may only have competences that fit within the framework of the constitution and their actions are limited to their own territories; the principles of state superiority and certain specific prohibitions on the actions of the communities uphold the principle of solidarity.

The principle of *equilibrium* seeks to guarantee a balance which provides support to the harmonized development of Spain. This requires a balance of economy among the various regions which might require action from the central state. The principle of *financial sufficiency* allows tax-raising powers at the level of the communities, although they may not raise taxes for matters beyond their territory or which would create obstacles to free movement of persons and goods. The principle of *non-federation* means that separate autonomous communities may not aggregate to form centralized units. However, communities may form agreements for mutual cooperation.

## Procedures for the Establishment of Autonomy

The constitution provides three routes towards autonomy. This multiplicity of routes is another reflection of the compromise that appeared necessary in the constitutional debate. Thus an express route to autonomy was provided for the Basque region, Cataluña and Galicia, these regions having already embarked on the road to autonomy in 1931. For these regions the constitution provided a route to full autonomy which commenced with the agreement of their superior pre-autonomous organ, followed by the drafting of their statute by an assembly of their parliaments, such draft agreed with the constitutional commission of the congress, then a referendum of the electorate in the provinces making up such territories and, finally, ratification by the full chambers of the parliament.

## The Express Route

An exceptional route allowing an accelerated procedure was provided by Article 151 of the constitution, which states:

> 1. It shall not be necessary to wait for the five year period referred to in Article 143(2) to elapse when the initiative for attaining self-government is agreed upon within the time limit specified in Article 143(2), not only by the corresponding Provincial Councils or inter-island bodies but also by three-quarters of the Municipalities of each province concerned, representing at least the majority of the electorate of each one, and this initiative is ratified in a referendum by the absolute majority of the electors in each province, under the terms to be laid down by an organic law.

Thus, under this procedure, the region obtains full autonomy immediately, provided the provincial councils offer their support, together with three-quarters of each municipal council, and that at least half of the electorate support the move in a referendum held in each province.

Under the express route, the creation of the statute of autonomy follows four phases. First, the government calls all the deputies and senators elected within the territory which intends to accede to self-government so that they are constituted in assemblies, and they create the plan of the statute by absolute majority. Secondly, once the project is approved, it is passed to the constitutional commission of the congress which examines it with the help of a delegation from the proposing assembly in order to determine by common agreement a definitive formula. Thirdly, if the agreement is reached, the resulting text is submitted to a referendum of the electoral body of the provinces within the territory of the planned statute and, if it is approved by a majority of the votes, it goes up to the *Cortes Generales* for its approval by the plenary group of both chambers by means of a ratifying vote. Once it is approved, the king sanctions and promulgates it as a law. Fourthly, if it does not reach the necessary level of agreement between the constitutional commission of the congress of deputies and the delegation of the proposing assembly, the plan of the statute proceeds like a *ley* through the *Cortes Generales*. Then the text approved by the *Cortes* is submitted to a referendum of the electorate in the affected provinces and, if it is approved by a majority, it will proceed to its promulgation.

Another form of access to full autonomy by which the strict requirements of Article 151 could be avoided was that by which a gradual process of autonomy would be complemented by a *ley orgánica*. This route was adopted by the communities of Valencia and the Canary Islands.

## The Ordinary Route

Article 143 provides:

> 1. In the exercise of the right to self-government recognized in Article 2 of the Constitution, bordering provinces with common historic, cultural and economic characterisitics, island territories and provinces with historic regional status may accede to self-government and form Autonomous Communities in conformity with the provisions contained in this title and in the respective Statutes.
> 2. The right to initiate the process towards self-government lies with all the Provincial Councils concerned or with the corresponding inter-island body and with two-thirds of the municipalities whose populations represent at least the majority of the electorate of each province or island. These requirements must be met within six months from the initial agreement to this effect reached by the local corporations concerned.
> 3. If this initiative should not be successful, it may only be repeated after five years have elapsed.

This procedure was envisaged as the normal route to autonomy and would require the provincial councils to exercise a positive initiative towards autonomy supported by the vote of at least two-thirds of the municipal councils. Under this route the autonomous status would be low, and subject to a transitional period of five years before such regions could proceed to gain full autonomy.

The plan for the statute of autonomy would be created by an assembly composed of the members of the *Diputación* and the internal organs of the provinces affected by the deputies and senators elected within them. Once elaborated, the project would be passed to the congress of deputies in which the *Ponencia* of the chamber would examine the text and the documentation passed to it to check that it had complied with the constitutional requirements. If these were complied with, the statute would be processed in the same way as a *ley orgánica*. Where there was a lack of compliance with the constitutional requirements this would be notified to the assembly that would have created it and the process would be suspended until the defects were put right. When approved by the congress of deputies, the project would be remitted to the senate in which it would be processed in accordance with the ordinary legislative procedure.

A singular system was created for Navarra and Ceuta and Melilla. Navarra had historically enjoyed more autonomy than other regions in Spain, having been an independent kingdom until the sixteenth century. During the civil war, Navarra offered support to Franco and was therefore able to maintain its ancient rights (*fueros*) and was uniquely able to raise its own taxes. The 1978 constitution granted to Navarra autonomous status along the same lines as that provided in the ordinary procedure and with the power to raise taxes. Navarra was also given the option of merging with the Basque region. Ceuta and Melilla obtained autonomous status in 1995.

In the short term, this variety of procedures would mean that there would be different levels of autonomy granted to different regions, but in the long term the intention was that their powers of autonomy would even out. This variety of routes to autonomy might be criticized as a confusing mixture and potentially discriminatory. However, all the territories have passed this phase of the autonomous process.

## The Statute of Autonomy

The statute of autonomy expresses and makes effective the autonomy which is recognized by the constitution, and provides the structural model which the constitution has laid out. The statute of autonomy is defined in Article 147.1 of the constitution as the 'basic institutional law of each Autonomous Community and the State recognizes and regards each Statute as an integral part of the legal system'. The statutes are self-regulatory and provide for the capacity to create their own rules, but are not an expression of sovereignty, since sovereignty resides in the state, as provided by the constitution. They have, in accordance with Article 147.1, a double significance: on the one hand, they belong to the legal system of their respective autonomous community, where they constitute a basic superior institutional rule, rather like a constitution of the autonomous community, and, on the other hand, they are an integral part of the state's legal system the regard and recognition of which they depend upon. The state recognizes their validity and treats the statutes of autonomy as an integral part of the legal system. From this hierarchical perspective they are subordinated to the constitution. They may stand against the rest of the law or, in other words, they cannot be modified by other laws because they are organic laws.

The process by which the statutes are created will determine their legal nature. Thus, for example, those created according to Article 146 are treated like a law created by the state parliament. Those created according to the procedures laid out in Article 151(2) however, appear, according to a number of commentators, to have a mixed nature between a territorial and a state law, while other commentators suggest that they are still really state laws since only the parliament has the power to approve them.

As noted above, the statute is drafted by the members of the *Diputación* of each province, that is the deputies and senators elected by the province which is to become the autonomous community.

What is the place of the statutes of autonomy in the hierarchy of laws? Under Article 81 of the constitution, statutes of autonomy are regarded as organic laws, giving them a superior place in the legal hierarchy, yet there are a number of complications which overwhelm this seemingly straightforward view. First, the statutes are approved in a different way to other organic laws and, secondly, the procedure for modifying them is also distinct, since they cannot be modified by another organic law, but only in the way provided by themselves. The autonomous communities' legal system and the state legal system are divided by the competences which fall within each system, so that in theory there is no room for the statutes of autonomy to conflict with state laws. However, the principle of integration between the systems complicates this theoretical assumption. Thus, from one hierarchical perspective, the statutes are subordinated to the constitution, yet, at the same time, they are immune from modification by a state law. This immunity comes from their treatment as basic or fundamental rules within the integrated system. Furthermore, they are created in a very formal manner, so that any less formal attempts to reform or modify or derogate them would not work. Article 147.3 of the constitution also provides a specific procedure for reform which does not include the possibility of derogation. Merino-Blanco (1996) suggests that the rules of the state system on matters which are within the jurisdiction of the autonomous communities are not abrogated, but remain applicable, although of a supplementary character. In Merino-Blanco's view, one could say that the Spanish legal system is made of a subsystem which is complete and general, and several partial and territorial subsystems which have a priority of application on the matters within their scope. Under Article 149(2) the state law is supplementary to the law created by the autonomous community. This rule recognizes the principle of autonomy.

The contents of the statute of autonomy are determined by Articles 147(2) and (3) and 152(1). Thus Article 147(2) states that the statutes must contain the name of the community that corresponds most closely to its historic identity; the delimitation of the community's territory; the denomination, organization and seat of the community's institutions; the powers assumed within the framework established by the constitution; and the bases for the transfer of services corresponding to those powers.

## Reform of the Statutes

Since all of the autonomous community statutes have been created, perhaps the more interesting issue today is that of their reform. The constitution does not provide in detail the formula for reform of these statutes. It does, however, make reference to the possibility of reform. For example, Article 147.3 refers to potential reform, as does Article 152.2, which provides for a special procedure. Each such article makes clear that the statute itself will have provisions for its own reform. In addition, Article 147 states that reform will require the approval of the *Cortes Generales* and Article 152.2 states that reform shall require a referendum of the people of the relevant community. All of the 19 separate statutes of autonomy contain rules for their reform and the following stages can be identified from them. Initiative for reform may come from the community's government or parliament, as well as the *Cortes Generales*, apart from the statute of Madrid. Some also allow for initiative to come from central government. Some also allow a percentage of the municipals to initiate the reform. All other forms of initiative are excluded. Parliamentary approval is required by all the statutes both initially, by the parliament of the community, and afterwards by the *Cortes Generales*, through a *ley orgánica*. Finally, the statutes approved by the special procedure add to the procedures the approval or ratification of the text by means of a referendum.

## Institutions of the Autonomous Communities

Article 152 of the constitution provides which institutions the autonomous communities will have and that these will be set out in the statutes of autonomy. Additionally, according to Article 152.2, each community will also set out in their statute the form and characteristics of participation in the organization of the judicial aspects of that territory.

Those territories which have full powers or which followed the exceptional route to autonomy have their institutions determined by the constitution in Article 152: a legislative assembly, elected by universal suffrage and arranged by a system of proportional representation, which assures the representation of different zones within the territory. The autonomous communities of the second grade have also established schemes which reproduce the scheme provided by the constitution for the first grade communities. In that way the second grade communities have a legislative assembly elected by universal suffrage with a system of proportional representation which guarantees representation of the different areas of the territory; a governing council which has executive and administrative functions; and a president elected by the members of the assembly and appointed by the king. The governing council is answerable to the president as the supreme representative of the community. The president and the members of the governing council will be politically answerable to the assembly.

The communities have therefore adopted the central government's characteristics, with a parliamentary form of government, with a separation of powers and control by the motion of investiture of the president and his or her political mandate over the governing council. The functions of the governing council are executive and administrative and this council has a president elected by the legislative assembly and appointed by the king. The functions of the president are to direct the governing council and to display his or her representation of the autonomous community and of the state within that autonomous community. Both the president and the members of the governing council are answerable to the assembly.

The third institution is the high court of justice of the autonomous community. Within the principle of unity and independence of the *Poder Judicial*, the *Tribunal Superior de Justicia* in each autonomous community represents the judicial body within the ambit of the territory. Thus actions begin in the courts of the particular territory in the first instance, without prejudice to the jurisdiction of the Spanish Supreme Court as a superior judicial body across all regions.

## The Autonomous Community's Parliament

All parliaments of the autonomous communities have only one chamber, comprising a variable number of members. These members are elected according to general electoral rules, except where specific rules are provided by the statutes. Members of the autonomous communities' parliaments have only a partial immunity for their actions. They may not be detained or retained, but in cases of proven criminal activity and any special offences they may be charged, imprisoned and processed by trial according to the *Tribunal Superior de Justicia* of the autonomous community and otherwise by the criminal court.

The parliamentary rules of each community determine the procedures by which sessions shall be run, as well as the length of parliamentary periods and the rules of the institutional organs. These rules are in a form similar to that established for the congress of deputies and senate of the *Cortes Generales*. The autonomous assemblies are dissolved by expiry of their term as well as by lack of appointment of a president of the community in the terms provided over a period normally of two months.

## The Autonomous Community's Executive

The president of the community is the highest representative figure of the community. He or she has competence to appoint and remove the members of the governing council, to direct the governing council and to coordinate its actions, and generally to give political direction as well as superiority to the autonomous community's administration. The role of the president is not compatible with any other public or private office. The governing council is a replica of the council of ministers at state government level and it carries out legislative functions as well as having powers of regulation, political direction, control of the administration and so on. The number of councillors is variable and, as has been noted, their appointment and dismissal depends on the opinion of the president.

## The Distribution of Powers

Autonomy is not the same as sovereignty. Each territorial organization granted autonomy is part of a whole and in no case can it use the principle of autonomy against state unity. Article 148 sets out the subjects in which the autonomous communities can assume powers and Article 149 establishes the subjects of exclusive state power.

The system of distribution of powers drawn by the constitution presents the characters of flexibility, variety with regard to the amount of autonomy, gradualism and agreement of the state. The different autonomous communities do not all have the same powers. As the constitutional court stated in 1981, unity is not the same as uniformity.

The exclusive powers of the state are reserved to regulation and the taking of decisions. These exclusive powers of the state are an irreducible, intangible and non-derogable nucleus of which the state cannot dispose. These are powers which correspond to the sovereignty of the Spanish people as a whole; they aim to maintain the ultimate unity of the legal and political system and are instrumental in assuring basic social homogeneity. The state is the guarantor and protector of the public interest. The autonomous communities, by contrast, may dispose of their autonomy for the management of their respective interests.

### Content of Article 149.1

The state has powers of legislation, regulation or execution over subjects which include nationality and immigration; international relations; defence and the armed forces; tax regulation; foreign trade; the financial and monetary system; public health; and the merchant navy. The state also has powers over various infrastructural sectors such as railways and public transport; works relevant to the general public interest; non-local civil legislation; and commercial, penal, sentencing and intellectual property legislation. Above this legislation the state has legislative competence and the autonomous community may assume the power of regulation and its execution or application.

## Powers Relating to the Autonomous Communities

The constitution neither defines nor guarantees directly a material breadth of powers specifically for the autonomous entities, nor does it fix the different levels of power which should be granted to each community. Both options are dependent on the acceptance of each community through the technique of the reserve to the relevant statutes. Article 147.1 states that the statutes of autonomy ought to contain, among other provisions, the powers assumed within the framework established in the constitution, and Article 148.1 says that the autonomous communities shall be able to assume powers and, after five years, and through reform of their statutes of autonomy, they shall be able to widen increasingly their powers within the framework established in Article 149. Paragraph 3 of Article 149 states that the subjects which are not attributed to the state by the constitution may fall within the competences of the autonomous communities by virtue of their respective statutes of autonomy.

The competences which are exclusive to those autonomous communities which followed the ordinary route to autonomy status are provided in Article 148; these competences include organization of their institutions of self-government; alterations of the municipal terms within their territory and, generally, the functions which are relevant to the administration of the state over the local corporations and whose transfer authorizes legislation over the local regime; territorial, urban and living organization of the territory; works of public interest within the territory; roads and railways within the territory; non-commercial ports and airports; agriculture and meatstock in accordance with general economic policy; the forests and countryside; environmental protection; waterways, fishing and hunting; local fairs; economic policy for the community; art and culture, local heritage, cultural research and teaching of the language where relevant; tourism, sports promotion; social welfare; safety and hygiene; and security.

## Shared Powers

There are two different ways in which the state and the autonomous communities may share their powers. First, the state might have legislative competence over a particular issue and the autonomous community have executive power over the matter. Alternatively, the state reserves the basic power of legislation and the autonomous communities may develop that by further legislation. In a sense, the basic laws are established by what is required by the public interest in relation to an issue. The basic laws are those which establish the principles and general rules which seek to ensure a minimum unity within the legal system. Legislative development implies a legislative activity which is free of political options and what this means is that the basic legislation establishes a general global system and within that system operates the normative powers of the specific autonomous community.

The shared powers include areas in which the state provides general framework legislation; areas in which the state has general legislative powers and specific elements, such as public security, are left to the autonomous communities; areas in which the state retains planning powers or defines the basic administrative policy of the sector, such as with the budget; areas in which the state is given a coordinating role over the autonomous communities, areas in which the state determines the economic parameters for public service management; areas in which the state retains certain managerial responsibilities, allowing other matters to be undertaken by the autonomous communities; and areas in which the state retains responsibility for public service, but not its management.

## Powers Delegated by the Autonomous Communities

It is possible to alter the system of powers defined by the statutes through a framework law or through an organic law. The *Cortes Generales* may attribute certain state powers to all or some of the autonomous communities; for example, the power to make their own orders and legislative rules in the framework of the principles, bases and directives issued by a state law. The state may transfer or delegate to the autonomous communities, through a *ley orgánica*, corresponding powers regarding those of the state which by their own nature might be susceptible to transfer or delegation.

The statute of autonomy may give power to the autonomous community to create legislation of its own. The legislation made at the autonomous community level is published both in the Official Journal of the Autonomous Communities and in the Official State Bulletin. It is also possible at the autonomous community level for *decretos legislativos* and *reglamentos* to be created.

## Tax-raising Powers

The resources of the Autonomous Communities are provided for in Article 157 of the constitution. These include taxes collected by the state; taxes and contributions of their own; transfers from the interterritorial compensation reserves and others assigned from the general state budgets; and money obtained from profits and assets arising from private law charges. The communities may not adopt tax measures for assets situated outside their territory or which pose an obstacle to the free movement or provision of goods and services.

## Harmonization Laws

The state can create laws that establish the necessary principles for harmonizing the legal provisions of the autonomous communities even in the case of subjects attributed to their own powers when this is considered to be in the public interest. This amounts to limiting autonomy and requires justification. Such justification may lie in the fact that it is a consequence of the principle of unity and of the supremacy of the national interest. Within the area of limitation of the powers of the autonomous communities, it is appropriate to consider the rules of harmonization provided for in Article 150.3. This article provides that the state will be able to create laws that establish the principles necessary for harmonizing the provisions of the autonomous communities even in the case of areas of competences attributed to those communities in so far as the public interest requires it. The majority of each chamber of the *Cortes Generales* will be responsible for this. This provision has been heavily criticized by the nationalist groups and by those who support autonomy, since it denotes a marked centralist orientation and at the same time is expressed in vague and ambiguous terms.

## Control of the Activity of Autonomous Communities

Control of the activities of the organs of the autonomous communities is exercised, in accordance with Article 153 of the constitution, by the following institutions: the constitutional court as regards the control of legal provisions with legal force; the government with prior order of the council of state, as regards the control of the exercise of the functions that the state should have delegated to the autonomous communities; the administrative courts, which have control of the legality of actions of the autonomous administrative bodies and their regulations; the accounts court, which has economic and budgetary control.

*Special Controls*

Articles 150.1 and 150.2 provide for controls of the exercise, by autonomous communities, of functions which have been delegated or transferred to them by the *Cortes Generales* or by the state. For example, where the *Cortes Generales* grant to the communities legislative powers which normally fall within the power of the state, those laws which grant such powers must also contain the means of control over those regional norms. Similarly, the government can impose controls where its powers are delegated to the autonomous communities. Another form of control is by the mutual duty between state and autonomous community to provide information about their activities.

*Exceptional Controls*

Article 155 of the constitution provides for extraordinary controls which force the autonomous community to comply with its obligations or to protect the public interest which has been put at risk by its actions. For example, this may occur in response to an insubordination or an attack on legality. The government may adopt the necessary means to allow it to achieve a strong execution of the obligations not complied with or the protection of the general public interest which has been threatened.

*Ordinary Controls*

The constitutional court exercises control of the constitutionality of the legal provisions that have legal force. Any challenge to the legal provisions must be based on constitutional rules. The *Cortes Generales* have power to authorize cooperation agreements between autonomous communities which are not concerned with provision or management of services. These latter simply require notification to the *Cortes Generales*. Finally, the national ombudsman has power to supervise administration of the communities and each community also has its own ombudsman.

## References and Further Reading

Alonso Zaldívar, Carlos and Castells, Manuel, *Spain Beyond Myths* (1993, Alianza, Madrid).
Cazorla Prieto, Luís María and Arnaldo Alcubilla, Enrique, *Temas de Derecho Constitucional y Derecho Administrativo* (1988, Marcial Pons, Madrid).
Constitución Española (1978), Title VIII.

*El Funcionamiento del Estado Autonómico* (1996, Civitas, Madrid).

García de Enterría, Eduardo, 'El sistema autonómico quince años después' (1994) 84 *Revista Española de Derecho Administrativo*.

Lopez Guerra, Luís *et al.*, *Derecho Constitucional*, vol. II, 3rd edn (1997, Tirant lo Blanch, Valencia).

Merino-Blanco, Elena, *The Spanish Legal System* (1996, Sweet & Maxwell, London).

Merino Merchán, José Fernando *et al.*, *Lecciones de Derecho Constitucional* (1995, Tecnos, Madrid).

Ministry of Foreign Affairs, *Autonomous Communities* (1994, Diplomatic Information Office, Madrid).

Serra, Narcís *et al.*, *Organización Territorial Del Estado en España* (1993, Universidad de Salamanca, Salamanca).

Torres del Moral, Antonio, *Principios de Derecho Constitutcional Español*, vol. 2 (1986, Átomo, Madrid).

# 8    Criminal Law

Spanish criminal law focuses on the protection of the individual and the community. Its historical development has been shaped by the political environment and changes from left to right which have occurred in Spain during the nineteenth and twentieth centuries.

## Codification in Criminal Law

The rise to power of Primo de Rivera in 1923 marked a turning point in Spanish politics in the twentieth century and initiated a new Criminal Code in 1928 which was more authoritarian than the liberal codes of 1868 and 1890. The 1928 code was more corrective. Then, in 1932, when the republicans gained power, a new code was created which showed signs of a humanitarian approach, highlighted in particular by the abolition of the death penalty. Then, in 1944, another code was created under the influence and leadership of General Franco which was, on the whole, authoritarian, although some humanitarian characteristics could also be found. That code also accommodated newly created offences of conspiracy, incitement and provocation.

In 1963, a new code was created and a number of changes were made to that code during the 1960s, with a further reform in 1971. The latter change included a recognition of the liberalization of religion so that the original offences against the catholic faith became offences against religious freedom, the state's religion and the other faiths. Further changes included the introduction of the offence of genocide after Spain joined the International Convention for the Prevention and Punishment of Genocide; other changes included offences against freedom and security at work. These changes finally came to fruition in 1973 when the revised code was published.

After the creation of the 1978 constitution, which reflected a move to democracy, a new approach to criminal law was adopted. The new constitution itself contains references to aspects of Spanish criminal law. For example, Article 25 states that it is only possible to be convicted for established crimes and Article 9 makes clear that penal provisions may not be applied retrospectively. Article 15 specifies that everyone has a right to life and physical and moral integrity and may not be subjected to degrading or inhuman punishment. The death penalty remains abolished except for cases of wartime military punishments. Article 25 also states that penalties which take away liberty cannot include forced labour but may be re-educative or rehabilitative.

Work for the creation of a new code began early – before the constitution was itself concluded. However, the new code was not completed until 1995 and did not enter into force until May 1996. The new Criminal Code is inspired by a democratic policy and is based on the principles of legality, culpability and minimal intervention. The principle of legality requires the application of security measures to be possible only where permitted by law. The principle of culpability is that there shall be no punishment without guilt. Article 20 also contains a number of conditions which are interpreted generally as exceptions from culpability or as non-culpability, such as physical defects, intoxication caused by dependence on alcohol or certain substances, or unsoundness of mind. Among the causes of non-culpability are included necessity where the harmful conduct is the best possible alternative conduct in the circumstances, or insuperable fear, or mistake as to the illegality of the action. The principle of minimal intervention focuses on punisment being the exception for acts of careless conduct. Thus these crimes tend to be very specific; examples are homicide as a result of serious negligence or abortion arising out of gross negligence. Another illustration of the principle of minimal intervention is that the preparatory acts of conspiracy, incitement and provocation are only punishable in specific circumstances. Furthermore, offences by omission are considered as exceptional.

Significant changes were made in 1995 to the penalties available against criminal conduct. Recognition of the negative effects of prison sentences is manifested by the fact that deprivation of personal liberty has been simplified into three categories: a prison sentence, house arrest at weekends, and personal liability for non-payment of fines. Under Article 36 of the new code, the maximum prison sentence is 20 years and the minimum sentence is six months. It is possible to replace prison sentences of less than one year with arrests at weekends or fines, depending on the circumstances. The idea of the weekend arrest is to avoid the corrupting effects of life in prison and such arrest is therefore conducted in solitary confinement. Other alternatives include fines or community service, although the difficulties with these are also recognized. Another new aspect of the 1995 law was the introduction of daily fines rather than fines which simply reflect the level of gravity of the offence.

Spanish criminal law is not only contained in the Criminal Code but also consists of a series of specialized criminal laws. Indeed, the Criminal Code is complementary to the specialist laws. One group of the specialist laws complements the provisions in the general part of the Criminal Code, for example the law which regulates trials of young offenders, or the laws which regulate prisons. There also exists a second group of specialist laws that establishes certain offences which are not contained in the code. These tend to be in areas that are subject to frequent changes, such as in air navigation. Finally, there exists a series of laws that have a wider content as well as being of an administrative, civil, mercantile or procedural nature. They thus supplement the rules already contained in the code.

## The Concept of Criminal Law in Spain

There are two schools of criminal law in Spain. From one perspective, Spanish criminal law is regarded as a system of social control by which the state, through a determined system of rules, can punish with negative sanctions those who deviate and cause harm, assuring necessary social discipline and socialization of the members of the group. That is the more dynamic and sociological view. An alternative, static and formal view is that the criminal law is a system of public law rules which define certain actions as criminal and associate with those actions penalties and security measures.

It is also interesting to note that the title of this field of law is *Derecho Penal* rather than *Derecho Criminal*. This has grown out of tradition and is no longer regarded as a polemical issue. However, García-Pablos (1995) considers that the conventional system has two advantages: the first is that it underlines what may be regarded as an offence and how that might be accompanied by a penalty and, secondly, the label *derecho penal* coincides with the view that no penalty may be imposed without a crime having first been committed.

## The General Part and the Specific Part of Criminal Law

In Spain, criminal law is divided into two major parts: the general part and the specific or special part. Effectively, the general part consists of the main principles and theoretical concepts of crime and punishment. This general part provides a framework for the specific part, which consists of the details of particular crimes and the rules relevant to those specific offences. The general part has a philosophical nature since it is constructed around a series of principles or theories which constitute the axioms of criminal law of all civilized systems. The general part also has elements which reflect current criminal law policy and, since it contains principles covering both crimes and penalties, it could be regarded as a complete and harmonized system.

One distinction that can be made between the general and the special parts is that the general part is non-specific and has no practically applicable rules. Such rules require to be elaborated upon within the special part to be given any practical effect. In other words, the two parts operate in a complementary manner to each other.

The general part contains the broad principles which accommodate the rules of the specific crimes. For example, the concept of 'culpability' is described abstractly in the general part of the Criminal Code. The specific part of the code, however, builds upon the general definition by explaining its application in the narrower context of each specific offence in question. The general part of the code also describes the concept of crime and punishment and reparation. Theoretical analyses of the general part of the criminal law also discuss how the criminal law relates to other areas of law, the various schools of thought within the field of criminal law, sources of criminal law and how a rule applies in terms of time and space. A second aspect of the general part is concerned with the theory of crime and what constitutes a crime from a general perspective, such as the part played by acts or omissions and the chain of causation, as well as what constitutes a defence. The specific part of criminal law describes particular crimes and what are the elements of those crimes, as well as the defences available and the relevant sanctions applicable.

Another difference between the two parts is that the general part may rely more on analogy, whereas the rules in the special part are more likely to be interpreted literally. It also seems possible for the general part to include customary rules, whereas this is unlikely to be the case for the special part which operates on the basis of no crime without law. This principle would appear to eradicate the possibility of recourse to custom as a direct legal source.

The specific part is rather fragmented and does not appear as an aggregate whole. However, the offences which are contained in the special part do appear to be ordered and classified and this allows the special part to have some degree of order and clarity.

## The Sources of Spanish Criminal Law

The Criminal Code, as well as other, complementary sources, has a very important role to play. The Criminal Code of 1995 provides a framework for the other rules which make up the system of Spanish criminal law. As was stated above, the Criminal Code of 1995 was influenced, in particular, by the promulgation and entry into force of the 1978 constitution, which assumed the establishment of a democratic legal system. Work was started on the reform of criminal law in Spain before the constitution itself was created, and afterwards various texts were created, culminating in a draft code in 1994 which became the 1995 code. The 1994 text was based on all the previous drafts, although in the interim period after the constitution had been created a number of reforms to the old criminal law were introduced. (Notably, the 1985 law reform partially decriminalized abortion.)

The 1995 Criminal Code has effectively brought the criminal law up to date and has adopted some of the Scandinavian approaches to sentencing, such as the introduction of a daily fine and of community service. Another modernization is the effective beginnings of a juvenile criminal law, since the code raises the age of majority from 16 to 18 years for the purpose of the application of the criminal law. However, provisionally, the age of 16 remains the age of majority for criminal law purposes and some critics note the lack of an infrastructure for an effective criminal law such as youth punishment centres or security measures appropriate to young people. The range of crimes in the Criminal Code reflects the modern age, including, for example, the crime of wrongful genetic modification.

As has already been noted, Spanish criminal law consists of more than the Spanish Criminal Code. Indeed, a number of different legal instruments together make up the Spanish criminal law. From this perspective, the following sources provide the Spanish criminal law. The *ley* will normally be a legal provision of a general character and reserved for the *ley* is the creation of criminal offences and the relevant sanctions in response to such crimes. Since a criminal law most drastically affects the rights and freedoms of individuals, Article 81 of the Spanish Constitution, which requires such law to be a *ley orgánica*, applies. Custom is also relevant. Even though specific offences cannot be created by customs, and nor can the corresponding sanctions, it is possible for certain justifications to arise from customs which are recognized in other areas of law. General principles are not normally applied directly but they are relevant to the interpretation given to the laws. Court decisions are not actually sources of law but they complement the law by interpreting the written legal provisions. They may become law in a negative sense by stating that a written provision or action is not constitutional, so that such written provisions cannot be applied or such actions cannot be pursued. Although the international treaties to which Spain has adhered have not actually prescribed specific crimes or criminal sanctions, they have created a number of principles which shape the internal criminal law, such as protection of ethnic minorities or respect for religious beliefs. The Spanish Constitution is also an indirect source of Spanish criminal law which does not contain specific crimes or sanctions but does

require such laws to be interpreted in conformity with constitutional principles and can determine as inapplicable any law that is created in breach of
the constitution.

## The Special Part of Criminal Law

As was noted above, Spanish criminal law is divided into two distinctive
parts: the general and the special. The special part concentrates on the more
specific and particular criminal law rules, which prohibit or mandate by
threat of specified sanctions actions or omissions. Broadly, while the general part is found in Book I of the Criminal Code, the special part can be
found in Books II and III, which refer to serious offences (*delitos*) and
minor offences (*faltas*) respectively. There are some exceptions to this general rule. The science and basic teachings are to be found in the general part.
Furthermore, it is important to recognize the unity which exists between the
two parts, the general part providing a framework and substratum for the
special part.

In reality, the special part of the criminal law has developed in a piece-
meal and fragmented fashion, which has prevented the creation of a system
as generic and abstract as the general part. However, there have been attempts to rationalize the special part so that a logical system can be achieved.
Thus some general ingredients for specific crimes have been identified.
These include the nucleus of the crime based on the conduct, then other
possible elements such as the result of the conduct, the means used, the
place and time of the conduct, qualifications, intentions, subjects and object.

Generally, the method of study of criminal law in Spain follows a three-
stage process: establishing the general framework; groups and subgroups of
types of offences; and analysis of each such offence. It may be possible to
classify offences in various ways, for example, as crimes against the person,
crimes against society or crimes against the state. Another method would be
to classify according to the type of right to be protected. Thus, for example,
crimes against life and bodily integrity would include homicide, wounding,
attempted killing, torture, genocide, crimes of danger such as traffic offences, crimes against public health, crimes against the environment, and
possession of arms and explosives. Offences against liberty and security
would include threats and coercion, resistance and disobedience, kidnap and
illegal detention, discovery and revelation of secrets, omissions of help, and
actions against other freedoms protected by criminal law. Crimes against
honour or reputation and privacy would include harm to such reputation,
contempt of court and revelation of secrets. Crimes against the family would
include crimes against the civil state, child stealing, abandon of the family

and children and actions against other protections of children. Crimes against the socioeconomic order would include workplace offences, tax fraud, black markets and money laundering. Crimes against property may include for example, theft, robbery, fraud, theft of a motor vehicle, illegitimate use of telephone equipment and infringement of intellectual property rights.

## The Concept of a Crime in Spanish Criminal Law

Article 10 of the Spanish Criminal Code, unlike some other European criminal codes, provides a definition of an offence (*delito*) as offences or faults, acts or omissions which are negligent or imprudent and punishable by the law. Article 13 offers some further clarification of these terms by stating that *delitos* are infringements that the law punishes with serious sanctions, *delitos menos graves* are infringements which the law punishes with less serious sanctions and *faltas* are infringements which are punished by light sanctions. Thus it appears that offences may be committed by positive actions or by omissions and they may be committed by negligent or imprudent actions. In order to constitute a crime, such acts or omissions must actually be punishable by sanctions already prescribed by the law.

## Penalties and Security Measures

Both penalties and security measures are legal consequences of harm done or potentially dangerous situations which arise. A penalty may be distinguished from other legal consequences by its preconditions and the procedure by which it is imposed. The necessary precondition is that an offence has been committed. Penalties are imposed exclusively by judges and criminal courts and by a determined procedure which is laid out in the *Ley de Enjuiciamiento Criminal de 1882* (Law of Criminal Procedure 1882).

The penalty may take a number of forms, ranging from imprisonment to suspension from employment and to fines or confiscation of driving licences. Finally, the penalty is notably the most serious of legal consequences because it is an expression of social reproach by the community towards the person who commits the offence. It is a form of retribution in response to culpable behaviour.

A security measure is more a preventive action which is conducted in dangerous circumstances. One problem is that security measures may be taken before an offence has been committed and from this perspective may be considered as marginal to the criminal law since they do not involve punishment. However, they are part of the criminal law and process since they are deemed to be 'pre-offence' measures: that is, measures taken prior to the commission of an offence. They may be imposed on individuals who are considered to be dangerous without requiring that they have committed a crime. This leads many theorists to argue that these measures belong, not to criminal law, but rather to the area of administrative law. The *Ley 16/1970 de 4 de agosto de Peligrosidad y Rehabilitación Social* (Law of 4 August 1970 Relating to Risk and Social Rehabilitation) adopts criminal law terminology and formally is treated as a criminal law. Thus, for example, it treats the following individuals as persons who are in a state of danger and applies to them security measures if they represent a social danger: prostitutes, vagrants, habitual alcohol or drug users, habitual liars, those who act in a cynical, insolent or brutal manner which puts the community or animals or plants in danger, and those who are part of groups or associations which have criminal objectives. The security measures which might be adopted include internment in custody or work or rehabilitation centres, weekend arrests, isolated quarters in alcohol-free houses, submission to vigilance by delegated persons, escorts, fines, and prohibition from residence in certain places or from visiting certain places. The law is criticized for confusing social danger with criminal danger, with predelictual measures being its essence. This law also puts into jeopardy the principle of no punishment without crime.

### References and Further Reading

Cerezo Mir, José, *Curso de Derecho Penal Español – Parte General*, 5th edn (1996, Tecnos, Madrid).

Cuello Contreras, Joaquin, *El Derecho Penal Español* (1993, Civitas, Madrid).

García-Pablos, Antonio, *Derecho Penal – Introducción* (1995, Universidad Complutense, Madrid).

Herrero Herrero, César, *Introducción al Nuevo Código Penal: Parte General y Especial* (1996, Dykinson, Madrid).

Luzón Cuesta, José María, *Compendio de Derecho Penal, Parte Especial* (1997, Dykinson, Madrid).

Muñoz Conde, Francisco, *Derecho Penal: Parte Especial* (1996, Tirant lo Blanch, Valencia).

Vives Antón, T.S. and Cobo Del Rosal, Manuel, *Derecho Penal – Parte Especial*, 4th edn (1996, Tirant lo Blanch, Valencia).

# 9    Private Law

Private law is defined by Ruggiero (1977) as 'the collection of rules that regulate relations between individuals themselves and between individuals and the state or other minor political entities which do not exercise functions of political power or sovereign power'.

In Spanish legal theory, private law may be contrasted with public law in the following ways: private law rights may be given up, while public law rights cannot be renounced; public law cannot be modified by individuals, whereas a private law rule may be modified or excluded by individuals who might dispose of a given rule voluntarily; when a public law rule is infringed the corresponding action is public and is exercised through either a criminal legal action or an administrative action; in private law it is the interested and injured party who must instigate a civil action in the civil law courts; subjective rights arising from private law are acquired and lost by prescription and by the passage of time, but public law rights cannot be extinguished in this way; private law demands the principle of autonomy and acceptance: it is the acceptance of interested parties that determines the legal relationship between them.

**Classes of Spanish Private Law**

There are two main branches of private law: civil law, which aims to regulate the natural person in his or her family and matrimonial relationships, and in his or her economic and property relationships; and mercantile law, which is concerned with commercial or mercantile activities and regulates the position of the commercial actor and his or her business relations. Local or *foral* law represents a third branch of private law, which is civil law relevant to certain specific autonomous communities.

## Civil Law

Castán Tobeñas (1991) defines civil law as

> the system of norms of a general or common nature which regulate the legal relationships of private individuals (individuals or collective entities) within an aggregated group, protecting the individual and his or her interests, as much from a moral perspective (rights of personality, family and corporations) as from a property perspective (sphere of rights of real property and of obligations, of inheritance and trusts and succession).

Civil law is a general law which tries to regulate all aspects of personality. It also contains branches of law which regulate specific aspects and activities of the person. Civil law also applies to mercantile law in situations where the Commercial Code makes special reference to civil law, otherwise known as common law. The civil law is concerned with natural personality from birth until death, dealing with the human person per se, that person's acquisition of legal personality, his or her capacity to work, and so on. Civil law is also concerned with the family and marriage, dealing with the contractual aspect of marriage and the personal and economic relationship between husband and wife, as well as the relationships between parents and children and matters such as affiliation. Another aspect of civil law is that of the property rights of the person, from two angles: the person's relationships with assets and chattels, real property, and the person's relationships with other persons, such as his or her rights as a creditor. Civil law also deals with hereditary succession. It is also concerned with the legal person (institutions and associations) which is granted the same personality, capacity and powers as the natural person.

*The Civil Code*    A primary source of civil law is the Civil Code of 1889. This code has several parts, the most important of which are the preliminary title and the four books. The preliminary title deals with the legal rule as a general norm and the sources of law. The first book is concerned with the person from birth and the creation of personality as well as paternal relations, blood relationships and the civil registry. The second book focuses on property and the transfer of property as well as the regulation of property rights. The third book centres on the different means of acquiring property. The fourth book is dedicated to obligations, understood as all relations of credit between two or more persons and contracts which are voluntary agreements made with the intention of establishing obligations.

## *Derecho Mercantil: Mercantile Law*

Mercantile law is the branch of private law which regulates the status of the business person and his or her mercantile, industrial and commercial activity, including also the capacity for being a commercial actor as well as the form of commercial activity. This area of law is concerned with the law of companies as regards, for example, the constitution and management of companies. Mercantile law is also concerned with commercial contracts and addresses issues such as the places and types of commercial transaction. Shipping law also falls within the realm of mercantile law.

The basic legal source of mercantile law is the Commercial Code of 1885. This code has a similar structure to that of its 1825 predecessor. The Commercial Code is complemented by other laws and rules such as the Law of Public Companies 1989 and the Law of Private Companies 1995; the Regulation of the Mercantile Register; the Law Relating to the Protection of Consumers and Users of 1984 and the Law on Cooperatives of 1987.

## *Derecho Foral: Local Law*

As has already been stated, local law constitutes the special civil law rules of a particular autonomous community. Certain Spanish regions have their own civil law. Such local laws are recognized expressly in Article 149 of the constitution. The character of local law is derived from the point in history when Spain was divided into kingdoms. Those territories with a local law include Vizcaya and Alava, Cataluña, the Balearics, Galicia, Aragón and Navarra. The other autonomous communities remain subject to the common civil law.

The local laws cover only specific fields of civil law and the Civil Code applies in the remaining fields. Thus Article 149 provides that the state has exclusive competence to regulate certain areas of civil law which, by reference to Article 13 of the Civil Code, may be identified as: all rules relating to the application and effectiveness of legal rules and sources of law; matrimony, apart from rules relating to the economic aspects of marriage; organization of registries and public documents; and bases of contractual obligations. In other areas of civil law, the local laws will apply and the Civil Code will act as a supplementary source of regulation. Another important aspect of the local laws is the local domicile by which a person identifies himself or herself as belonging to a specific territory and this is normally determined by family connection. For example, a married woman normally adopts her husband's domicile and minors follow that of their father, or that of their mother.

The next section will provide a brief outline of the process of codification by which the Civil Code (as well as the Criminal Code and the Commercial

Code) was created. A description of the Civil Code will then follow before a summary of the basic rules relating to persons, contracts and obligations in Spanish private law.

## The Codification Process Leading to the Civil Code

Spain was not alone in experiencing a process of codification. Across Europe there was a sharp expansion of legal rules which contrasted with the stability of the Roman law. This inspired a need to bring together into a rational order all the different rules that had been created over time; the need to systematize and add certainty to the mass of different laws that had grown in the so-called 'Modern Age', together with the technical idea that equality before the law could only be achieved by the existence of a single law common to all and taking away the privileges and exceptions which had characterized the law of the absolutist period. The French Revolution adopted this approach and this gave rise to the creation of the Napoleonic Code of 1804. However, it could be argued that the codification process has earlier roots, such as in Spain with the Ninth Recompilation under King Carlos IV. From the early nineteenth century, codes were created across Europe. The aim seemed to be to tie the hands of the judges to the discipline of the laws. Napoleon had said that the judge is no more than a reader of the law to be applied, but in contrast there appeared to be a failure to recognize the plurality of the different territories, each with their own rules.

In Spain, codification took off around the beginning of the nineteenth century. The Ninth Recompilation was the first attempt to organize and then put into an order the dispersed legislation of the Bourbons. The work failed to be implemented as a result of the French invasion and subsequent events. The next real steps towards codification began in 1821, when a commission was set up to draft a Civil Code. Again, this work was a victim of the political events which took place and another attempt was not made until 1851. The 1851 initiative for the creation of a Civil Code faced opposition from those who wanted to maintain the regional laws and, because of the slow development of the project, there emerged a number of sectorial laws relating to specific areas, such as the *Ley de Hipotecaría* (law on mortgages) and the *Ley del Registro Civil* (law on the civil registry). These specific laws put an end to the possibility of a broad-based civil law code.

The continued struggle for recognition of the local laws was a formidable obstacle to the creation of a unified code. One attempt to resolve this problem came in 1880, with a royal decree which ordered there to be local representatives in the general codes commission and the carrying out of a series of reports and studies on the local foral institutions which still had a role at the time. It emerged that in reality there were few significant differences between the Castilian laws and the local laws, except in the areas of hereditary succession and matrimonial property. After a failed earlier attempt in 1881, there was approved in 1888 a *Ley de Bases* which authorized the government to draft and publish a Civil Code in accordance with the conditions, directives and bases established in that *Ley*. Importantly, the *Ley* made it clear that the Civil Code would be a supplementary law to the local laws, thereby fully preserving the application of the local laws. A draft Civil Code finally appeared in 1888 in the *Gaceta de Madrid*. This draft became the Civil Code of 1889, which still forms the basis of the civil law in Spain today.

The Civil Code of 1889 was clearly influenced by the French *Code Civil* of 1804, as is revealed by its principles and structure, but another clear influence was the local laws which would remain applicable as a result of the concessions granted in the final code. For example, the rules on succession reflect the foral laws and different compilations were eventually made for each of the areas with foral laws. Other matters that have either influenced the code or helped to form an appropriate interpretation of the code include the Italian and Portuguese codes, as well as custom, doctrinal theory and jurisprudence.

When the Civil Code was created it was not intended to create a whole new law. The code was instead limited to regularizing, clarifying and harmonizing the laws already in existence and only where new circumstances gave rise to a need to introduce new rules would this be a part of the new code. Another characteristic of the code is its recognition of individualism: for example, the deference to property rights, at times at the expense of the social solidarity necessary in certain situations.

As was noted above, the code contains four books relating, respectively, to persons, property and the transfer of property, different modes of acquiring property, and finally, obligations and contracts. Some areas which might be expected to have been accorded a separate book within the code are instead dealt with within the existing books. For example, there is no distinct book providing rules on the family. Instead, this is dealt with partly in the book relating to persons and partly in the book relating to obligations and contracts. Similarly, succession is dealt with in the third book as one of the modes of acquiring property.

There exist a number of criticisms of the code. Many of these are a consequence of the codificatory process itself; for example, the code was executed too slowly, and the appearance of new sectorial laws meant that the code was not a comprehensive legal source. The question of local laws and how they fit into the system also remains. The continual need to revise and modify the code is a further problem. Other criticisms of the code are that it lacks a general part or any informative criteria and that it has technical defects and an old-fashioned approach. On the other hand, the scientific approach to the code makes it a more logical document than the French code.

Overall it can be argued that the code has a central role in providing a systematized starting point for the civil law. Since the code contains rules with a general application, it is regarded as a general legal text rather than just as a civil law source. It has application to private law generally, as well as to some aspects of public law such as for procedural issues. In some ways the code might be regarded as a form of common law since it applies generally and also acts as a supplement to the local foral laws. The political significance of the code is that it represents nineteenth-century liberal and individualistic ideology. In this way the code highlights the basic and fundamental right of property and establishes the freedom of contract as a basic principle, declaring that contractual terms are to be determined by the contracting parties. The code is also conservative and pays little attention to social structure; it seeks to preserve the traditional laws which already exist, rather than to change them radically.

**The Law of the Person**

Personality is the legal qualification necessary for enjoying rights and fulfilling obligations. The regulation of personality is found in the first book of the Spanish Civil Code. According to the code, birth and death constitute the existential limits of the person. The definitions of both birth and death are purely legal rather than biological and are concerned with the practical effect these have for the enjoyment of legal rights and obligations.

The code is also concerned with legal capacity which is itself an attribute of personality since it signifies the person as a subject of legal rights and duties. In Spanish law there are two levels of capacity: legal capacity by which the person is the holder of rights and duties, and capacity to act by which the person is able to exercise rights and carry out his or her duties. It is thus recognized that an individual may not be capable of effecting his or her rights or duties, for example, as a result of his or her age or mental capabilities. In these circumstances it may be necessary for the person to have a legal representative or guardian in certain situations. Under Article 12 of the Spanish Constitution, the age of majority is 18 years and the age of majority generally signifies the move to full legal capacity unless the individual has certain disabilities such as illness or insanity which makes them unable to perform their duties or exercise their rights independently. Until individuals reach the age of majority their capacity to act is limited. Thus they may not enter into certain legal relationships. For example, they may not obtain a financial loan, or obtain a mortgage for buying real property or commercial or industrial establishments or objects of extraordinary value, without the consent of their parents. Where they are able to enter certain legal relations this requires them to have gained 'emancipation' either by law such as through having married, or by obtaining parental consent or the consent of the court. Where a minor is emancipated he or she may be tried in court.

Where a person has not reached the age of majority and has not been emancipated, he or she cannot exercise their rights of their own motion, nor can they be expected to fulfil their duties. Instead, their parents will be responsible for them. The parents also have certain duties towards their children, such as the duty to protect the child and to keep them in their custody as well as to provide them with necessities such as food and education and to administer the property of their children. If there are no parents or there is a parental failure, the child will have a guardian who will carry out their functions under the control of the *Ministerio Fiscal* and the protection of the courts.

Another aspect of personality which is particularly relevant to Spanish law is that of domicile and a person's civil law vicinity which determines which laws will govern the individual where foral and local laws are relevant. Generally, an individual will adopt the same civil law domicile as his or her parents. Where the domicile of the two parents differs, the child will normally adopt the domicile which has been determined for him or her beforehand or, failing that, it will be the place of the child's birth; and failing that, it will be the vicinity of the common law. A child who is 14 or over can opt to adopt the vicinity of his or her birthplace or the last vicinity of his or her parents. It is also possible for one spouse to adopt the vicinity of the other spouse.

## Contract Law in Spain

The fourth book of the Civil Code of 1889 covers obligations and contracts. One of the main sources of obligations is the contract. From one perspective, the fact that obligations can be created out of a declaration of intentions between two or more parties is a manifestation of free will. It is possible to argue against this point when it is clear that some contracts are not so freely entered into by all the parties and at other times one party has a much stronger bargaining position than the other. Nevertheless, the starting point in the civil law in Spain is that, since the contract is an expression of freedom, it should have legal effect. The Civil Code does not actually offer a definition of contract, but basically it is understood to be a common agreement between two or more persons on a practical proposition, which the contracting parties remain bound to each other to observe.

Mere consent between the parties actually forms the contract. However, the Civil Code makes it clear that a contract must have certain essential elements, without which there would not exist a contract. Article 1261 of the Civil Code states that there is no contract without the following: consent of the contracting parties, a material object and a cause for the obligation. Consent is manifested by the combination of offer and acceptance regarding the object and cause which constitute the contract. It is also made clear that consent must be given freely and consciously and with full capacity for giving such consent. Thus non-emancipated minors cannot give consent, nor can persons of unsound mind or deaf and dumb people who do not know how to write. Nor should the consent be granted as a result of error, violence, intimidation or threats. The object of the contract is the giving of something by the obligation of one party to the other. The object must be possible, legal and determined or determinable. The cause of the contract is effectively the objective such as a contract of sale by which an article is given in return for money. Again, the cause must be lawful.

The form of the contract is not regarded as an essential element of the contract. However, this general principle is limited since there are some contracts, such as the provision of immovable property, which require to be in writing.

## Obligations in Private Law

An obligation is a credit relationship between two or more persons, from which arises a group of rights and obligations for each person involved. According to Article 1088 of the Civil Code, an obligation consists of giving, doing or not doing something. By virtue of an obligation, a person ought to give something to another or do something for another or, indeed, not do something.

Every obligation has a double facet: an active and a passive aspect. The active comprises the content of rights that arise for one of the parties in the relationship, to whom he or she is called a creditor, and the passive comprises the rights that are exercisable for the debtor for whom arises an obligation in which he or she must give something, do something or provide a service, or omit to do something. In other words, the obligation supposes the existence of two determined parts: a creditor and a debtor. The creditor has the right to demand from the debtor a specific thing or to require the debtor to do or not do something and the debtor is obliged to observe the relevant conduct.

In each obligation there are three elements: a subjective element which is either active (creditor) or passive (debtor) and which can be individuals, collective groups, natural or legal persons; an objective element in which the object is to give, to do or not to do something and the object must be legal, possible and identifiable; and a legal relationship or a nexus between two or more persons.

### The Sources of Obligations

Obligations can derive from contract, or from causing harm or other various causes of law. The Civil Code, in Article 1089, states that obligations are created by law, by contracts or quasi-contracts and by illegal acts or omissions in which there is an element of fault or negligence. Unilateral acceptance may also create an obligation, but this is debateable because it does not appear as one of the conditions in Article 1089. Article 1090 states that the obligations derived from the law cannot be presumed since it is not possible to take these for granted. A contract is a voluntary agreement which gives rise to an obligation. Article 1091 states that obligations created by contracts have legal force between the contracting parties. Quasi-contracts are legal actions which are purely voluntary and unilateral, with the result that they bind the actor to a third party and sometimes there will be a reciprocal obligation between them both. An illegal act is an action which contravenes the law and consists of a harmful action carried out in bad faith that produces an injury for others and a breaking of the law. Fault or negligence can include non-contractual actions as well as indirect responsibility: for example, that of the father for the action of his sons.

### Classes of Obligations

The fourth book of the code, chapter III, includes the following classes of obligations: pure and conditional, time limits, alternatives, joint and collective, divisible and indivisible, and obligations with a penalty clause. Pure obligations are defined by Article 1113.1 of the code. Compliance with these is necessary from the moment they are created, as the code states that 'it shall be necessary whatever the whole obligation whose compliance does not depend on some future or uncertain event or on a past event'. Conditional obligations depend on a future and uncertain event of which there are two types. The first type is a suspended condition which leaves the effects of the obligation in suspense: for example, 'I have no obligation if you do not win the race'. The second type of conditional obligation ends when a condition is complied with: for example, 'If you win the race you will not have to clean my house.' Obligations for a time limit exist where the creation of an obligation is left to a future occurrence but it will have to be met even though it is not clear when. Article 1125.2.3 of the Civil Code states that it is understood that a certain day means that it will come, although it is not certain when that day will come. If the uncertainty consists in whether or not the day will arrive, the obligation is conditional. For example, the day of the election is a time limit which may suspend the obligation or it may bring the obligation to an end. The election will suspend the obligation if it is not necessary to pay until the election, alternatively the condition may be that you must work until the election, at which date the obligation to work ends. In that case the day will definitely come, although it is not known when. Until that day arrives, compliance with the obligation cannot be demanded, nor can the debtor be freed from the debt. Alternative obligations require the debtor to comply by carrying out various possible actions. The debtor can choose its form, although the choice might also be given to the creditors.

## Collective Obligations

Collective obligations are characterized by having a number of debtors or creditors, or both. A group of debtors or a group of creditors does not necessarily require action by every person. These obligations are presumed to be divided equally under Article 1138 of the code. For the obligation to be divided, it is necessary to have a divisible object. If the object is indivisible, the debt becomes effective against all the debtors and if one debtor cannot pay the others will be obliged for his or her part, but they may receive an indemnity from him or her.

## Joint Liability (obligaciones solidarias)

In these cases, all the debtors have responsibility for the whole debt. The creditor may demand from an individual debtor the compliance of the obligation for all the objects. Each debtor must provide wholly the objects of the obligation and each creditor may receive the whole. In such cases the debtor who paid may reclaim from his or her co-debtors the part which corresponds to each of them. When one of the debtors pays the whole debt this extinguishes the obligation, but another is created in which the debtor who paid becomes a creditor of those who were his or her co-debtors. Similarly, the creditor who receives the whole becomes a debtor of all his or her prior co-creditors. Generally in Spanish law, there is a presumption of jointness but not a presumption of solidarity. That normally only exists where expressly provided. Where there is solidarity between debtors, the creditor may demand the payment or action from any one of them or from all of them simultaneously.

## *Divisible or Indivisible Obligations*

Divisible obligations are those that can be complied with partially and in different parts or stages. Indivisible obligations cannot be complied with in distinct parts. A divisible obligation is frequently an obligation of doing something in a number of days of work or works by distinct units.

## *Obligations with a Penalty Clause*

There are three types of penal obligation: a liquidatory demand as compensation for harm or prejudice; a sentence or fine; and power of the creditor to demand compliance with the obligation. These penalty clauses have a coercive function or a guarantee function together with a liquidatory function. It is not necessary to demonstrate prejudice except for non-compliance with such a clause.

## *Obligations Arising as a Result of Negligent Actions*

Article 1809 of the Civil Code makes a clear distinction between legal, contractual and quasi-contractual obligations, on the one hand, and, on the other hand, obligations which arise from illegal acts or omissions or in which there has been involved fault or negligence. Article 1902 states that anyone who by action or omission causes harm to another, involving fault or negligence, is obliged to make reparation for the harm caused. The individualistic nature of the provision in the Civil Code is founded on the economic and social conditions in which the code was drafted. These consisted of individual relations in a non-industrial but agricultural and artisanal society and one in which the law aimed to moralize the conduct of individuals rather than to assure victims of compensation for harm they have suffered. The emphasis was more on payment for wrongdoing than on compensation for injury experienced. Another factor of some importance was that the kind of society which existed with relations being between individuals rather than involving complex organizations meant that the cause of injury was easy to establish.

Spanish economic and social conditions have become as complex as those of any other industrialized society and this has given rise to the need to modernize the law. Thus, while the Civil Code still provides the basic principles, these have had to be developed by the courts and the legislature in order to take account of complex modern society. Consequently, the need to compensate persons for injuries caused, for example, by the risks inherent in developing industrial processes and which do not necessarily involve fault or negligence, has been recognized. In the same context, it has become necessary to accept that responsibility does not necessarily fall on one individual, but that it may be more appropriate to require compensation to be made by a collective body. This need arises partly because of the complexity of modern processes in which there may be a number of possible causes for harm suffered. Even if one individual can be identified as the primary cause, it may be that that individual has acted as part of a chain of events leading to the harmful occurrence. Spanish law has had to deal with the reality of social and economic modernization and a number of legislative provisions and court decisions reflect that reality. Before looking at some of those changes, it is appropriate to outline the basic characteristics of civil responsibility in Spanish private law.

According to Díez-Picazo and Gullón (1997), civil responsibility can be classified according to different circumstances. First, it is necessary to distinguish between subjective and objective responsibility. Subjective responsibility is based exclusively on fault, while objective responsibility arises independently of all fault. Thus subjective responsibility may arise out of my failure to adopt the correct safety precautions when operating a machine. Objective responsibility might arise out of accident. Secondly, responsibility may be direct or indirect. Direct responsibility is imposed on the person who causes harm as a result of his or her own actions, while indirect responsibility is imposed on a person who has not actually caused the harm but the harm has arisen as a result of another's actions. Thus indirect responsibility might fall on an insurer. Thirdly, it is possible to distinguish between principal responsibility and a subsidiary responsibility. A principal responsibility can be pursued in the first instance whereas a subsidiary responsibility arises when the principal defendant owes no duty or cannot comply with the responsibility.

Díez Picazo and Gullón also identify four essential elements of a non-contractual civil responsibility. First is a form of conduct which may be either an act or an omission. In other words, it is a human action which might consist of a positive action or a negative action, omission or abstention. Unlike the situation in the area of contractual obligation, the act must be unlawful in order for there to arise the responsibility; the Civil Code does not demand illegality, but states that the act or omission must involve fault or negligence. This has not been clearly defined and it is suggested by commentators that, in the area of civil responsibility, fault or negligence may be defined broadly. The second element which is necessary to establish civil responsibility is that the action or omission has resulted in harm or injury. The harm must be real and not hypothetical or a mere possibility, but it may include a future harm if that is certain, such as the certainty that an individual will require an operation in two years' time as a result of injuries caused by a negligent act. The types of harm recognized for the purpose of civil responsibility fall into two broad categories: harm to property and moral harm or harm to the person. Property harm may include, for example, damage to material assets or interference with a debt. Injury to the person may include bodily harm or interference with an individual's rights, such as damage to a person's reputation or interference with a person's privacy. The third element of civil responsibility is the existence of a causal link between the action and the harm suffered. This requirement may be difficult to establish when there exist complications such as influence of outside forces or acts of third parties intervening in the chain of events, or contributory fault of the person who suffers the injury.

The final essential element of civil responsibility is that of fault which must be established on the part of the actor who is identified as having caused the harm. The law has evolved dramatically in this aspect of obligations in order to take into account the change in philosophy from focusing on the moral obligation to pay for wrongful actions to focusing on the need to protect individuals and ensure that victims are compensated. This change in philosophy has led the Supreme Court to move from the principle that the victim must prove that the defendant acted with fault to a presumption of fault on the part of the defendant requiring him or her to prove that they acted with all the necessary diligence. Such developments appear to clash with the constitutional principle, stated in Article 24.2, of the presumption of innocence until proven guilty. This point has been answered rather unsatisfactorily by the Supreme Court in its argument that the person who causes the harm and is presumed to be at fault is not being punished or sanctioned but is merely being asked to compensate for harm caused by his or her actions.

Fault or negligence are defined in Article 1104 of the Civil Code as the omission of that diligence required by the nature of the obligation and corresponds to the circumstances of the individual as well as time and place. Diligence obliges a person to adopt the measures necessary to avoid the resulting harm, so long as this is foreseeable. The individual is negligent if he or she does not do what needs to be done to avoid the harmful result or has not taken adequate measures to avoid that result. According to Article 1104, paragraph 2, where the specific measure necessary to achieve diligent conduct has not been defined the standard against which the individual's conduct is to be measured is that of the *buen padre de familia*. Essentially, this means the standard of a prudent head of household, corresponding more to English law's idea of a reasonable and prudent man, rather than a caring parent. In other words, the individual must show the level of diligence which would be displayed by a normal or average person.

Another type of conduct which does not strictly fall within the category of fault or negligence but which also gives rise to civil liability is *dolo*, when the actor knows that his or her conduct will or is likely to provoke injury and he or she does nothing to avoid that result. In these circumstances, although the harm is not intended, it appears as a necessary consequence of the action. Whereas liabilities which arise out of fault or negligence may be exonerated by the person who suffers the harm, this may not be allowed for harm caused by the *dolo*. *Dolo* is treated as intentional wrongdoing which may include a reckless course of conduct or gross negligence thus bringing the concept closer to the criminal law.

Another aspect of responsibility relates to that of responsibility for the acts of third parties. Article 1093 of the Civil Code states that a civil, non-contractual obligation may arise, not only from one's own acts or omissions, but also indirectly, as a result of the acts or omissions of others. Article 1093 provides a specific list of those who could be held liable for the acts or omissions of others, but the same article adds that they will not be held liable if they applied the diligence of a *buen padre* in order to prevent the harm.

Those who may be held responsible for the acts or omissions of others include the parents in whose custody the child may be; legal guardians of minors or disabled persons; employers; and school teachers of children under the age of majority during the periods in which those children are under the control and vigilance of the school and are engaged in curricular and extracurricular activities. Individuals may also be held responsible for the actions of their animals, and specific rules also exist for persons who own dangerous or ruined buildings. It is also possible to be held liable for industrial activities which are recognized as dangerous or noxious. Specifically, the Civil Code lists the following in Article 1908: explosion of machines which have not been cared for with the due diligence required and the inflammation of explosive substances which were not placed in a secure or appropriate place; excessive emission of noxious fumes; the falling down of trees at a roadside as a result not of unforeseen circumstances such as the tree being struck by lightening; and emission of substances from sewers or of infectious materials caused as a result of being built without the necessary precautions. Finally, specific laws have been created to deal with certain activities which are recognized as dangerous. Such laws include the Law relating to the Use and Trade of Motor Vehicles of 1968 and amended in 1986; the Law of Air Navigation of 1960; the Law relating to the Protection of Consumers and Users of 1984; and the Law relating to Product Liability of 1994, which was created in order to implement the EC Directive, 374/88, of 25 July 1988.

# References and Further Reading

Albaladejo García, M., *Compendio de Derecho Civil* (1995, Bosch, Barcelona).
Broseta Pont, Manuel, *Manual de Derecho Mercantil*, 10th edn (1996, Tecnos, Madrid).
Calvo Meijide, Alberto, *Introducción al Derecho Público y Privado* (1994, Prensa y Ediciones Iberoamericanos, Madrid).
Castán Tobeñas, José, *Derecho Civil Español, Común y Foral*, 10th edn (1991, Reus, Madrid).
*Código De Comercio y Legislación Complementaria* (1996, Dykinson, Madrid).
de Ruggiero, R., *Instituciones de Derecho Civil* (1977, Reus, Madrid).
Díez-Picazo, Luís and Gullón, Antonio, *Sistema de Derecho Civil* (1997, Tecnos, Madrid)
Montes Penades, Vicente, *Introducción al Derecho Civil* (1995, Tirant lo Blanch, Valencia).
Olivan López, Fernando, Ezquierra Serrano, María de Rosario and Muñoz Blasquez, Fernando Manuel, *Introducción al Derecho*, 3rd edn (1993, Tecnos, Madrid).
Uría, Rodrigo, *Derecho Mercantil*, 23rd edn (1996, Marcial Pons, Madrid).
Vicent Chuliá, Francisco, *Introducción al Derecho Mercantil*, 9th edn (1996, Tirant lo Blanch, Valencia).

# 10  Procedural Law

## The Concept and Characteristics of Procedural Law in Spain

Procedural law is a group of norms that regulate the requirements and the effects of the legal process. Against the concepts of jurisdiction and of action understood as the right to effective judicial protection, the concept of process appears as the projection of a whole group of demands of a different type, but fundamentally social and legal, that have made necessary the birth of the law of procedure. According to Moreno Catena *et al.* (1995), procedural law is an instrumental law in so far as it protects not only the rights of individuals but also all parts of an organized social community. The role of procedural law is to provide legal protection and thus to give certainty and security to relations and legal situations. Procedural law is also a category of public law partly because the procedural rules direct the role of the judicial organs which are themselves organs of the state. This has the consequence that the procedural rules are mandatory: it is not possible for the parties to derogate from the procedural rules.

Procedural rules may be limited in time or in space. The rules could be changed over time, making it difficult to know which are the applicable rules, the old or the new. However, transitional rules often deal with these difficulties. As regards space, the state or the *Cortes Generales* have exclusive competence to create procedural legislation, without prejudice to the special needs created by the existence of the autonomous communities. The rules created by the *Cortes Generales* extend only as far as the national territory and so the procedural rules apply only within the Spanish territory, and those rules which refer only to a specified autonomous community will apply in that community only. Conversely, rules created outside Spain are not applicable within the Spanish territory.

Spanish procedural law has four main branches: civil process, criminal process, labour law process and administrative law process. The civil law process covers all private law relationships, including mercantile law. Other means of resolving private disputes may be through arbitration. The civil law process is mainly written, dispersed and with little application of the principle of *inmediación* – immediate effect. The main criticisms of the current civil law process are that it is too liberal, and allows the parties too much control, with the effect that there is little confidence in the truth of the evidence presented; there are too many formalities which are not appropriate to the modern environment; there have grown too many different possible procedures, so that there is a danger of making a mistake; finally, the judge may be absent for much of the process, which may lead to a number of corruptions.

The criminal process involves the requirement of a process by which a sentence may be delivered. It is necessary to have a process which achieves some proportionality between the crime and the sentence and which recognizes the individual circumstances of each case. The criminal process is normally preceded by a preparatory phase of instruction or summary. The main observations about the current criminal process are that the preparatory phase is too long and thus is difficult to justify against the principle of the presumption of innocence. The judge who instructs must not pass sentence or give a judgment.

The administrative process is intended to offer a means of appeal against administrative acts similar to the system of judicial review in the UK. However, it is regarded as inadequate since the system depends on the willingness of the administrative body to comply with the decisions of the court, which cannot be guaranteed.

The labour law process is a special civil law process which takes account of the sociological demands of the workplace and employment relationships. Thus it is a much speedier system and less formal. The magistrate is present at all stages and directs the process. There are problems because some regard the process as lacking in seriousness and lacking in guarantees but, on balance, it appears to be regarded more positively than the other processes.

## The Sources of Spanish Procedural Law

From among the legislative acts promulgated by the *Cortes Generales*, the main source is the constitution. Article 5.1 of the *Ley Orgánica del Poder Judicial* affirms that the constitution is the supreme norm within the legal system and that it binds all the judges and courts. Those rules that appear in the constitution and which refer to procedure will have immediate application. The rules that appear in Articles 117 to 127 of the constitution and which concern the *Poder Judicial* determine and specify the form that the process shall take. It is in the ultimate control of the courts and judges. Ramos Méndez (1992) suggests four reasons why the constitution should be regarded as the primary source of procedural law: first, because there are identified within the constitution the values which preside over the organization of society among which are expressly cited justice and liberty; and secondly, because there are established in the same way the fundamental guarantees that must preside over the system. Specifically, Article 24 of the constitution states that all people have a right to obtain effective protection of the judges and courts in the exercise of their rights and legitimate interests. The article goes on to say that everyone has a right of access to the courts, the right to a defence and the assistance of a lawyer, to be informed of an accusation made against them, to a public process and not to testify against themselves, as well as the presumption of innocence. The third reason for the constitution's supremacy, according to Ramos Méndez, is that the constitution establishes the basic structure of the system which can be regulated by the *Poder Judicial* independently of the other state powers. Fourthly, the rules of the constitution may be applied directly by the judges and courts. This is confirmed by Article 5 of the *Ley Orgánica del Poder Judicial*.

Besides the constitution, the procedural system is guided by another important group of norms. On the one hand, there are the procedural laws which regulate the organization of the jursidiction in different courts. There is also the procedural activity of the parties, independently of what is found in the procedural codes or the substantive laws. On the other hand, there are normative provisions which regulate each type of trial in the different jurisdictions.

Together with the constitution, other sources of procedural law include laws promulgated by the *Cortes Generales* such as any *ley orgánica* or *ley ordinaria*. By contrast, neither rules created by the executive nor custom are to be considered as sources of procedural law. One reason that custom is not considered to be a source of procedural law is that it does not come from the legislative body and also custom tends to be relevant to a particular place. Therefore, if customs were to be admitted, it would mean that there would be different procedural laws throughout the national territory.

There exist a number of basic laws that form the nucleus of Spanish procedural law besides other general rules contained in the Civil Code and the constitution. These laws include the Law of the Judiciary, 1985 (amended in 1997), the Law of Civil Procedure, 1881, the Law of Criminal Procedure, 1882, the Law of Administrative Litigation Procedure, 1956 and the Law of Labour Procedure, 1990.

## Law of the Judiciary

The most important organic law is the *Ley del Poder Judicial de 1985* (LOPJ) which refers to the infrastructure of the judiciary. This regulates the territorial organization and the composition of the judicial organs and defines the mode of operation of the judges and courts. It also regulates the work of the civil servants and other personnel within the service of administration of justice. The LOPJ develops Title IV of the constitution, which is also concerned with the *Poder Judicial*. In this way it tries to accommodate the organizational scheme of the justice system to the constitutional demands and to the different social changes which Spain has experienced as well as to the new distribution of territorial power. The LOPJ aims to give practical support to the theory of the rule of law by which an institutional body or structure is required to enable individuals to protect their legal rights against abuse by others.

The LOPJ comprises a preliminary title and six books which refer to the different organizational aspects of the justice system. The preliminary title contains the basic principles by which the justice system should operate, including independence, immobility, submission to the law, responsibility as well as direct application of the constitution, interpretation of laws in accordance with the spirit of the constitution, prevention of fraud, and effective protection of rights and legitimate interests. The six books concern the following: extension and limits of the jurisdiction and the design and organization of the courts and tribunals; the government of the *Poder Judicial*; the regime of the courts and tribunals, that is the rules by which they operate; the code of the judicial personnel which governs the career of court workers; persons and bodies which cooperate or assist in the administration of justice, such as the fiscal ministry, lawyers, procurators and judicial police; and personnel who work in the administration of the justice system, such as legal secretaries, officials, forensic scientists and other agents.

This law has been developed and complemented by other laws concerned with criminal trials as well as the demarcation and design of the judiciary. The Law of Demarcation and Judicial Organization, 1988, defines the geographical space that corresponds to each judge and establishes the number of courts and servers in each judicial organ. A wider reform was introduced in 1994 which affected various different aspects, including the selection and formation of the court personnel, the rules of disciplinary responsibility, competences and regulatory power of the general council of the *Poder Judicial*.

### The Law of Civil Procedure

This law dates from 1881 and contains the rules on the voluntary jurisdiction as well as regulating three ordinary declaratory processes, various specialized processes and different routes for appeals. This law was modified in 1984, although with little success. It also forms the basis of the other provisions of procedural law within the civil law sphere. The law is divided into three books. The first book contains provisions common to both the contentious and the voluntary procedures. The second book deals with the contentious procedure and the third book deals with the voluntary procedure. Despite its length of 2182 articles, the law still leaves many aspects unaddressed. The law has faced many criticisms and has been modified by various different laws. Ironically, the centenary of the law began with alterations, since these were concerned with efficacy of the system. The 1984 law modification introduced some extensive reforms and was based on the principles of equality of the parties to the process. Basically, the civil law process has been criticized severely for its complexity and inefficiency. The need to refer to various specific laws beyond the law on civil procedure makes the system inefficient and difficult to apply.

## The Law of Criminal Procedure

This law dates from 1882. The criminal trial is basically divided into two parts: the summary part, which is mainly an inquisitorial process, and the oral hearing, which is accusatorial and public by nature. A number of reforms have been introduced over the years which have largely retracted from the liberal stance of the law as it was created in 1882. Furthermore, the introduction of the constitution in 1978 led to the criminal procedural law being interpreted in a different manner and, according to Ramos Méndez (1992), this marked the destruction of the law. The subsequent laws have had to be read alongside the 1882 law, with considerable difficulty, such as to lead commentators to regard the system as unworkable.

## The Law of Administrative Litigation Procedure

This law dates from 1956 and promotes the protection of the interests and rights of citizens against illegal acts of the administration. According to Ramos Méndez, this law itself may be regarded as modern and imaginative, although in practice it has been applied in a routine manner. However, the introduction of the constitution and the new territorial organization of the state have led to a need to introduce a new legislative text. The reality is that it is not so much the citizen but the administrative bodies that use the law. Furthermore, the law does not equip courts with the means to resolve modern administrative problems.

## The Law of Labour Procedure

This law was introduced in 1995, replacing an earlier law dated 1990. It is generally regarded as more effective than the other procedural laws which exist for other areas. On the other hand, some argue that it has mistakenly taken on aspects of the *Ley Orgánica del Poder Judicial*, establishing a parallel regulation. However, the law has the benefit of being relatively simple. At the same time, some prefer to use means of resolution outside this system, such as by agreements in the economic or labour law field.

*International and Community Law*

The contents of some international treaties and European Community law may affect the procedures adopted in the Spanish courts as in other national courts. For example, they may have an impact on extradition processes. Further, the Spanish courts are bound by the decisions of the European Court of Justice. Article 10.2 of the constitution demands that the rules concerned with fundamental rights and freedoms be interpreted in accordance with the Universal Declaration of Human Rights and the treaties and international conventions which are concerned with such rights.

**The Court System**

A brief outline of the institutions of the *Poder Judicial* was provided in Chapter 3 above. At this point it is appropriate to describe the different courts and the hierarchy of the court structure.

In order of the lower courts to the higher, the civil law courts include the *Juzgado de Paz*, which hears very minor claims, the *Juzgado de Primera Instancia e Instrucción*, which hears most civil claims at first instance and the *Audiencia Provincial*, which will hear appeals deriving from decisions of either the *Juzgado de Paz* or the *Juzgado de Primera Instancia*. The *Tribunal Superior de Justicia* has first-instance jurisdiction over civil cases which involve members of the autonomous government or parliament or patents and trade marks cases where the defendant is domiciled in the relevant autonomous community. The *Tribunal Superior de Justicia* may also hear appeals on decisions of the *Audencia Provincial*. The decisions of the *Audiencia* may also be appealed in the *Tribunal Supremo*.

It is appropriate to note the *Audiencia Nacional* which has jurisdiction to hear matters of national interest, such as extradition proceedings or crimes against the Crown. This is a collegiate court and hears cases in administrative, criminal and labour law, such as national collective bargaining disputes. In criminal law it hears cases such as those concerning drug trafficking, money laundering and terrorism. It also hears appeals against decisions by the *Juzgados Centrales de Instrucción*. In administrative matters the *Audiencia Nacional* reviews acts or decisions of ministers and secretaries of state. This court has been involved in considerable controversy over recent years as a result of its high profile political corruption cases.

Other civil courts include the *Juzgados Centrales de Instrucción*. These have national jurisdiction and, as well as carrying out the instruction stage for the *Juzgado Central de lo Penal*, they also do this for the *Audiencia Nacional*. *Juzgados de lo Social* have jurisdiction over employment contracts and social security. *Juzgados de lo Contencioso-administrativo*, in theory, will have jurisdiction over administrative matters. These have not yet been created, and such matters are currently heard by the *Tribunal Superior de Justicia* within the relevant autonomous community.

The criminal law courts include, from the lowest to the highest, the *juzgados de menores* which have jurisdiction over both criminal offences and the supervision of educational or other orders over minors. The *Juzgados de lo penal* hears allegations of offences committed within the territory of a province and also hear cases in which the offence is punishable by less than six years' imprisonment or by smaller fines. The *Juzgado Central de lo Penal* has national jurisdiction and hears allegations of crimes against the Crown and so on but for which the punishment of such offences would be less severe than for those tried by the *Audiencia Nacional*.

*Juzgados de vigilancia penitenciaria* are normally seated in the capital of each province and have jurisdiction over the enforcement of criminal penalties which involve loss of freedom, as well as protecting the rights of prisoners.

The *Audiencia Provincial* hears appeals from the decisions of the lower courts (apart from the *juzgado de vigilancia penitenciaria* and the *juzgados centrales*). Appeals against decisions of the *Juzgado Central de lo Penal* are heard by the *Audiencia Nacional* which also has first-instance jurisdiction, as described below.

The *Audiencia Provincial* also has first-instance jurisdiction over serious crimes.

The *Tribunal Superior de Justicia* may hear actions provided for in the *Estatutos de Autonomía* as well as over *instrucción* and judgment of actions against judges and fiscals. Appeals against decisions by the court can be heard by the Supreme Court – the *Tribunal Supremo*.

Finally, the Constitutional Court is separate from the organ of the *Poder Judicial*. The function of this court is to interpret the constitution and provide a control over parliament's exercise of its legislative powers. The constitutionality of decisions of the executive and the judiciary are also within the jurisdiction of the Constitutional Court. It is also the function of this court to protect the fundamental rights and freedoms provided in the Constitution of 1978, as well as to rule on the distribution of powers between the state and the communities.

## Principles of Procedural Law

*Good Faith and Loyalty of the Parties*

The LOPJ, in Article 11, states that facts illegally obtained will have no effect and imposes on the courts the obligation to reject petitions, incidents or exceptions which are formulated out of an abuse of the law or entail fraud of law or process. This is a principle which seeks to protect the public interest which would be ridiculed if the parties used the legal process fraudulently or were to seek results illegally. Article 48 of the statute of lawyers imposes on the lawyer the obligation to be prudent, loyal amd truthful in relation to the courts.

*The Principle of Effectiveness*

This is an important principle which requires the process to come up with a useful result. Effectively, it is a requirement of proportionality and this includes the aim of offering a proper solution, a reasonable duration, a reasonable cost and the facility of compliance with or execution of the results.

*The Principles of Duality, Equality and Contraction*

These principles refer to the position of the parties in the process. Duality indicates that there must be two or more parties; equality means that the parties are given the same opportunity of allegations, resources and so on; contraction signifies the right to be heard and the possibility of defending oneself.

*The Principle of Apportioning Control in the Conduct of an Action*

The legal process can be used by the parties in the sense that they have the power to initiate a legal action, to determine its contents and to conclude it. This principle is qualified, since the process is disciplined and controlled and the judges have their own powers of control. The principle of the law and the courts apportioning control of legal action to each party means that each party has a chance to incorporate into the process its own evidence and to present the corresponding proof.

*The Principle of Freedom of Evidence*

Generally, the evidence may be free and evaluated freely, but not arbitrarily.

## *The Principles of Procedure*

The trial is usually oral and the principle of publicity generally means that the procedural acts are public, as demanded by the constitution. However, there are exceptions for reasons of security, public order or respect for privacy.

## The Different Types of Process Available

The whole procedural law system contains processes which may be described either as declaratory or as executory. The declaratory procedures have the objective of making a declaration of the existence of a subjective right or legal relationship, to modify it or to constitute it or annul it or to require a debtor to comply with the right in some way. The declaratory processes may be classified as ordinary, summary or special. They may fall into categories of public and private law, the public law categories including the criminal process, the constitutional and the administrative, and the private law processes being the civil and the labour law processes.

### *The Ordinary Processes*

The ordinary processes tend to be wide-ranging, offering several possibilities to the parties in order to resolve their dispute. The parties have broad scope in the allegations so that all possible avenues may be exhausted. However, one resulting problem is that the ordinary processes are long and costly.

### *The Special Processes*

These are accelerated procedures which are intended to avoid some of the problems which arise from the ordinary processes. They apply to specified situations and may only be used for those particular issues. It is open to the defendant party to oppose the use of such procedures.

### *Summary Processes*

These processes are also designed to overcome the problem of delays in the ordinary processes. They are only available for certain situations and cannot be used at other times. Furthermore, the decisions which arise from such processes do not have a material effect on the parties.

## The Criminal Process

This process is an accusatory process and may be initiated by the fiscal ministry, a private prosecutor or the public prosecutor. The defence may be conducted by the defendant and his or her defence lawyer.

There are two phases in the criminal process: the instruction and the oral hearing. The first phase, the instruction phase, is where the judge receives instructions and has the function of preparing the case for trial. The judge must make investigations and take precautionary measures which may often involve a limitation or invasion of certain fundamental rights, such as the right to privacy, which may be breached as a result of the judge's investigations. The second phase is that of the oral hearing. Within the criminal process, and in conformity with the seriousness of the alleged crime committed, there are three ordinary processes and some special processes. The ordinary processes are called 'summary ordinary' in recognition of crimes with sentences of more than 12 years. In these the judge is instructed and a trial takes place in the *Audiencia Provincial* (provincial court). The other ordinary processes include the abbreviated criminal procedure with prior evidence given to the judge and with an oral trial either in the lower criminal courts (for crimes carrying a penalty of up to six years in prison) or in the *audiencias provinciales* courts (for crimes with a penalty of between six and 12 years in prison) and finally trials of minor offences, to be heard by the lower courts. Special processes are rare and depend on the person accused, for example a magistrate or member of the parliament, or on the type of crime involved, such as terrorism.

## The Administrative Process

The administrative process is regulated by the Law of Administrative Litigation Procedure of 1956. Trials take place in review courtrooms within the superior courts and within the Supreme Court. The 1956 law also introduced the concept of special lower administrative courts, but these have not materialized. The judicial review procedure may be used against administrative acts as well as against regulations and other provisions created by the administrative bodies. Under this procedure, such acts or provisions may be annulled or opposed and it is also possible to act against administrative personnel with the effect of having them removed. It is also possible to seek by this procedure compensation for harm or losses suffered. There is always a declaratory aspect of the decisions granted by this procedure such as an annulment or a condemnation of the administrative body concerned. There are one ordinary process and five special processes within the administrative law field.

## The Constitutional Process

The constitutional processes are regulated by the constitution and the organic law of the constitutional court. These procedures are governed by the principles of disposal, writing and single instance. They fall into two major groups: the protection of fundamental rights and the constitutional control of legality. For the protection of fundamental rights, it is necessary first to exhaust all earlier possible procedures. It is a form of appeal for special protection and must be initiated within 20 days of the last decision obtained in the lower court. The process involves the protection of rights as well as the creation of legal doctrine which may then guide the decisions of the lower courts. The constitutional control of legality has three possible procedures. The first of the procedures is that concerned with conflicts of competences which can be instigated by the state or by the autonomous communities. The constitutional court will be asked to decide which party has the competence in question. Another procedure is the abstract constitutional control by which a new law can be challenged for breaching the constitution and in order to secure the principles of supremacy and constitutional hierarchy. The third possible procedure, similar to an Article 177 reference before the European Court of Justice, is the specific control in situations where it is uncertain whether a law should be applied to a given case.

## The Labour Law Process

The labour law processes take place in the social section of the court system such as the *Juzgados de lo Social* or the *Sala de lo Social* of the Supreme Court and are regulated by the *Ley de Procedimiento Laboralde 1995*. The labour law procedure is regarded as less costly and more speedy and operates on the basis of principles such as oral hearing and double instance. A variety of issues can be dealt with under the labour process, such as requests to clarify a particular workplace relationship by determining the status of the worker, or to force the other party to comply with the agreed terms of the employment contract – for example, to re-engage an employee who had previously been dismissed. The labour process may be used for resolving individual or collective labour disputes.

The main features of the labour process are that it is conducted orally and that it focuses on the material facts at issue, thereby allowing the process to be conducted swiftly.

*The Civil Process*

There are various possible types of civil trial, and these cover such areas as matters within the Civil Code, mortgages and industrial and intellectual property. Generally, civil processes are heard by courts of first instance (*Juzgados de Primera Instancia e Instrucción*) or by the *Tribunal Superior de Justicia*, depending on the value of the claim or, in some cases, on its nature. The *Andiencia Nacional* has jurisdiction over matters of national interest such as crimes against the Crown or extradition proceedings. The courts at this level will not make a declaration. Appeals are taken to the *Andiencias Provinciales*, and a final appeal may be heard by the *Sala Primera de lo Civil* of the *Tribunal Supremo* (Supreme Court). The process is informed by the principle of sharing the evidence and the judge must remain passive until the facts have been established. There is considerable opportunity for the parties to distort the position and the whole process is slow, drawn out and costly. It is also very formalistic.

To deal with the delays inherent in the ordinary procedures, a number of special procedures have been established which now total at least 30 and in themselves make a confusing and inefficient system.

**The Trial**

According to Ramos Méndez (1992) there is no single applicable trial model. Indeed, the system is designed to protect citizens in a whole range of situations requiring that they be able to opt for the most appropriate formula for their circumstances. This has led to a wide range of special procedures that complement the ordinary procedures. However, Ramos Méndez argues that a modern system should seek to achieve one model that can be used in all cases. In any event, there exist some elements which are common to the structure of all trials within the broad sphere of procedural law.

A first structural level identified by Ramos Méndez is found in the declaration and execution, both of which are typical processes within a model of trial. Secondly, he identifies the phases of initiation and development of a trial from which arises the opportunity or necessity of the process being continued until its conclusion. Within this aspect there are the phases of preparation of the trial, the allegations, the evidence, the conclusions and the challenge or appeal. Finally, he identifies an aspect in which there is the possibility of repeating before a tribunal the debate about a legal problem. This refers to instances or grades of jurisdiction.

## The Declaration and Execution

These two phases establish whether or not there exists a right. It is a process in which the parties may introduce litigious questions. In some cases the mere existence of a judicial resolution is sufficient to complete the legal protection, but sometimes the decision requires a complementary action. It may be necessary to do this by means of a phase called 'execution' by which the judge makes an order for the compliance and protection of the right under threat or violated.

## Initiation and Development

*Preparation of the trial*   In any model of trial there exists a preparatory phase. This is, in reality, a phase of strategic preparation such as copying basic documents, locating important witnesses and so on. In this phase some actions, such as an attempt to conciliate between the employer and worker before bringing about the trial, may actually be legally required.

*Allegations*   This is the phase of collecting the facts to be presented at the hearing. In this the parties have complete freedom since they are participants who are in possession of the relevant information. The person who is making the allegations must seek to establish the facts that help his or her case, whereas generally the defendant is under no obligation to seek facts which positively justify his or her position. However, it would help his or her position more if he or she could show evidence which positively helped them. This phase also consists of the right to be heard and to counter the allegations made. The parties may present to the court different versions of the dispute. This may include the accusation and the reply, which may be an admission, a denial or an allegation of new facts or exceptions.

*The evidence*   This is the phase in which the alleged facts are verified to the court. It is necessary to distil the results which are controversial arising from the allegations. There may be presented confessions, witnesses, documents and evidence of judicial recognition. The judge has to evaluate the results during this phase of the trial.

*The conclusions*   Once again the parties and the judge offer a summary of the evidence. The system reserves to the judge the right to give the last word and his or her decision ends the debate. It is also possible to conclude the trial by other means, such as by a settlement or by a withdrawal by one party of the allegations.

## Appeal

This phase is a second opportunity to review the first trial. There are two possibilities: one of the parties may ask the same court to reconsider, or by petition a party may appeal to a higher court to review the decision of the lower court. Where the appeal is possible, this may be referred to as a multiple instance or a second instance. In administrative cases there is often only one instance, but otherwise there are at least two instances possible. A third possibility refers to a review of the law, but not of the facts. It is also possible to reopen decisions where they have been reached as a result of fraudulent representation of facts.

## Costs

One of the basic principles of the constitution is that of free access to justice. However, the reality is that justice has to be paid for and it is considered by many that the users of the system ought to pay for it. This raises the issue of costs. The general costs principle is that the costs must be met by the party who incurs those costs, although a number of special rules also apply. For example, in criminal procedures, costs normally fall on the condemned and where there is no conviction the state should meet those costs.

It is possible to modify the position on costs by agreement between the parties. For example, in a contractual agreement there may be a clause relating to costs. This possibility arises from the principle of freedom of contract contained in Article 1255 of the Civil Code. Some legal modifications to the general rule may apply, such as in matrimonial disputes in which the judge may order a certain proportion of costs to be paid by the parties.

The criteria to be applied by the courts in assessing the costs include the subjective criterion which is based on the conduct of the litigant. Additionally, the objective or the victory criterion suggests that the costs should fall on the loser. This arises out of the doctrinal opinions that the conduct of the parties is difficult to evaluate for the purpose of costs. A third criterion is that of the reduction of the costs in order to prevent potential litigants from being discouraged for fear of the costs that will be incurred. For example, Article 523 of the Law of Civil Judgments of 1984 suggests that, when the loser is required to pay the costs, these will be limited to the costs of the lawyers, experts and other functionaries that are not subject to tariffs. The total amount should not exceed for each party a third of the quantity of the process, up to a million pesetas. A fourth criterion is that of causation, by which the party who instigates costs unnecessarily, for example the vexatious litigant, shall be required to pay them.

According to Article 119 of the constitution, justice shall be free when this is provided for by the law and in every case for those who do not have enough resources for litigation. This is basically offered to those who have less than double the minimum salary and such costs exemption has to be obtained through a special judicial procedure. When the exemption is granted, the benefits obtained are exempted from payment of the evaluated costs. The party also has the benefit of free insertion in official newspapers of notices and edicts, exemption from making deposits that might be necessary for maintaining resources, and appointment of a lawyer and procurator without obligation to pay them honorary sums.

It is also worth pointing out, at this stage, that there are some important features relevant either to civil or criminal trials.

Civil proceedings are adversarial, and the parties are in control of the proceedings. There are various types of trial within the civil process, which largely depend on the amount of the claim. Thus claims over 160 million pesetas (approximately £80 000) follow the *juicio de mayor cuantía*, claims of under 160 million but over 800 000 pesetas follow the *juicio de menor cuantía*, claims of between 8000 to 800 000 pesetas follow the *juicio de cognicíon*, and claims of up to 8000 pesetas follow the *juicio verbal*. The *juicio verbal* is decided by the *Juez de Paz*. Since 1984 the most widely used type of procedure has been the *juicio de menor cuantía*. This procedure is also used for those cases where it is not possible to ascribe a fixed value, such as disputes relating to capacity or status or paternity suits. The *juicio de menor cuantía* is less formal than the *juicio de major cuantía*.

Criminal proceedings also have some characteristics worthy of note. For example, offences may be classified into 'public' criminal offences, 'semi-public' offences and 'private' offences. Such classification will determine who should proceed with the prosecution. Most offences are prosecuted by the public prosecutor – the *Ministerio Fiscal*. Semi-public offences require a prior report by the victim before the public prosecutor commences with the prosecution. These include such offences as rape or domestic violence. Private offences do not involve the public prosecutor.

The court with jurisdiction to hear a case depends on the importance and severity of the punishment which corresponds to the offence, as well as the capacity of the person alleged to have committed the offence. Very minor offences are tried by the *Juez de Paz* whereas minor offences are tried by the *Juez de lo Penal* in the locality of the offence or by the *Juez Central de lo Penal*. The *Audiencia Provincial* hears cases of in which the alleged offence carries a penalty of more than six years' imprisonment.

The nature of the procedure will vary according to the type of crime or dependant. For example, special proceedings apply for young offenders who will be tried by the *Tribunal Tutelar de Menores*.

Another notable aspect of the criminal procedure is that the possibility of an appeal on the merits of the case is not available where the case has been heard by the *Audiencia Provincial* or by the *Audiencia Nacional*. It is only possible to appeal on a point of law or procedure against the decisions of these two courts. It is possible to appeal against the decisions of the *Juez de Paz*, the *Juez de lo Penal* and the *Juez Central de lo Penal*. A *recurso extraordinario de revisión* may be possible when new facts show that the person has been wrongly convicted – for example, as a result of false documents having been earlier used as evidence.

It is also relevant at this point to note that jury trials were introduced in Spain in 1995 by the *Ley Orgánica del Tribunal Jurado*. Jury trials are limited to crimes against human life, crimes of the omission of duty to help, crimes against freedom, crimes against the environment and crimes committed by civil servants. The jury trial may only take place in the *Audiencia Provincial*.

Unlike in the UK, where there are 12 jurors in England and Wales and 15 jurors in Scotland, Spain's jury trial system allows for nine jurors whose role is to declare whether or not the facts are proven.

The jury trial relates more to the right of citizens to participate in public matters and in the administration of justice than to the right of the accused to be tried by his or her peers.

## Reform of Procedural Law

Procedural law in Spain is criticized widely for its failure to meet the needs of the social community and it is clearly in need of reform. It is largely ignored because people prefer to avoid legal technicalities and it is also feared because of the uncertainties involved in the litigation process, as well as the heavy costs. The reforms suggested by Ramos Méndez are more than formalistic reforms of the legislation. They are more fundamental, in that they focus on the role of the judge and the training and regulation of the judiciary and the advocacy profession.

## References and Further Reading

de la Oliva Santos, Andrés and Angel Fernández, Miguel, *Derecho Procesal Civil* (1991, Editorial Centro de Estudios, Madrid).
de la Oliva Santos, Andrés *et al.*, *Derecho Procesal Penal* (1992, Editorial Centro de Estudios, Madrid).

Lozano-Higuero, Manuel Pinto, *Introducción al Derecho Procesal* (1990, Ministerio de Justicia).

Merino-Blanco, Elena, *The Spanish Legal System* (1996, Sweet & Maxwell, London).

Moreno Catena, Victor, Cortéz Dominguez, Valentín and Gimeno Sendra, Vicente, *Introducción al Derecho Procesal*, 2nd edn (1995, Tirant lo Blanch, Valencia).

Ramos Méndez, Francisco, *El Sistema Procesal Español* (1992, Bosch, Barcelona).

# 11    Spain and the European Union

## Spain's Entry into the European Community

Spain entered the European Community in the second enlargement in 1986. The process of entry for Spain was long and difficult, her first steps being taken in 1962. The first enlargement of the European Community had centred on economic issues. By contrast, the second enlargement, which eventually brought into the Community Spain, Portugal and Greece, was predominantly political. Tsoukalis (1981) offers at least three reasons for the political emphasis: that politically, it was almost impossible to exclude any European democracy prepared to adopt the *acquis communautaire*; membership of the Community was seen as a factor of stability and as a means of strengthening parliamentary democracy; and political stability would, in turn, be a prerequisite for economic and military security.

Initially, Spain hesitated between joining the EEC and joining the European Free Trade Association (EFTA). The EEC became the favoured option because of the long-term political objectives of the Treaty of Rome and its attention to agricultural issues. Spain requested that negotiations be opened with a view to examining the possibility of establishing association with the EEC in 1962. At first, this request was greeted by silence because of the Community's attitude to the dictatorship of Franco. President de Gaulle had favoured Spain's entry in so far as this would extend the Community's influence southwards. However, farming issues stalled the negotiations which opened in 1967.

In 1970, agreement was reached on a preferential agreement between Spain and the EEC. This agreement was designed to conform with General Agreement on Tariffs and Trade (GATT) rules that preferential agreements must lead, in time, to a customs union. About 95 per cent of EEC industrial imports from Spain subject to tariffs were covered by the agreement and 62 per cent of agricultural imports, while approximately 61 per cent of Spanish imports from the Community were affected. The agreement was based on reciprocity. Following the accession of Denmark, Ireland and the UK to the EC in 1973, a temporary protocol covering Spain's trade relations with the three new European Community member states was signed in January 1973. The first enlargement meant that Spain's 1970 agreement needed to be renegotiated, since Spain had previously enjoyed free trade access to Britain.

In 1975, negotiations on a new agreement broke down following civil unrest in Spain and the execution of five men accused of killing policemen and civil guards. The executions were said to violate the rule of law and the rights of defence. The European Parliament had decided to freeze relations in September 1975 'until such time as freedom and democracy are established in Spain'. In December 1978, a multilateral free trade agreement between Spain and the EFTA countries was initialled. Bilateral agreements were also reached, with Spain and all of the EFTA countries except Iceland and Portugal, to facilitate trade in agricultural products.

Meanwhile, after the death of Franco in November 1975, King Juan Carlos committed himself to the 'peaceful establishment of democratic coexistence based on respect for the law as a manifestation of the sovereignty of the people'. The idea of a free trade association had become obsolete and Spain wanted full membership. Support for full membership came from all three major political parties. Spain's first general elections since 1936 took place on 15 June 1977, after which the government of Adolfo Suarez González agreed to submit a formal application for full membership of the European Community. Spain applied in July 1977, mainly on the basis of political factors, as a source of support in preserving her democratic institutions. The end of international isolation was seen as a reward for restoring democracy. The growing Spanish economy looked towards Europe; the Spanish people regarded Francoism as too primitive and political democracy became the aspiration. Fernando Morán, the then foreign minister, saw the completion of the accession agreement as recognition for having re-established democracy.

By 1977, economic, rather than political, issues had become the most important. This caused difficult entry negotiations. In the first place, there was French doubt as to the likelihood of full membership being achieved for Spain or Portugal before the end of 1983, as had been hoped. This was partly because France wished to resolve the problems which had arisen from the 1973 enlargement of the Community, such as the dispute arising fom the Community budget reform commitment.

The crucial question for the negotiations with Spain concerned agriculture, which was regarded as a threat to the economies of France, Greece and Italy. Spain's accession would increase the agricultural area of the community by 30 per cent and its farm work by 25 per cent, as it would increase the production of vegetables and fresh fruit and olive oil. Spanish wine also represented almost a quarter of Community output. Other serious issues regarding the prospective Spanish entry were fisheries, since there was an imbalance between the size of existing fishing fleets and the amount of available fish stocks, with Spain possessing the third largest fleet in the world, and trade barriers for Spain's industrial goods.

The new socialist government, which took office in December 1983, pledged to seek membership within four years, despite continued French objections to Spain's entry into the Community. The Accession Treaty was finally signed on 12 June 1985, with Spain entering on 1 January 1986, at the same time as Portugal. The main terms of agreement for Spain's entry included the following: customs duties to be dismantled in eight stages over a seven-year transition period, duties being reduced by 50 per cent by 1989 and abolished by 1993; quantitative trade restrictions to be abolished from the date of accession, although Spain was given between three and four years to phase out import quotas on certain sensitive products, such as tractors, colour televisions and guns; market access for some textile exports was to be subject to a programme of double checking and statistical surveys of existing member states' imports; for agriculture, a seven-year transition period would generally apply for the implementation of the Common Agricultural Policy and for some products this would be extended to 10 years; for most fish the alignment of price differences and dismantling of customs duties would take place over a seven-year period, and Spain and Portugal would have to conform to EC rules on minimum fish sizes, fishing gear, catch limits and quotas; and Spain to receive pre-accession aid for restructuring its fleet. With regard to institutional arrangements, Spain would have eight votes, while the UK, France, Germany and Italy were to have 10 votes. These agreed terms showed that there had been relative inequality of bargaining power between Spain and the Community, the end result not being very generous to Spain.

Since Spain's entry into the European Community, she has gained considerable economic improvements. During 1997 the *Financial Times* was reporting that economic figures looked positive, with Spain seeking to qualify for the European single currency. Growth was edging up and inflation was at its lowest for a quarter of a century. More jobs were being created and there was a narrowing of trade gaps as well as the balance of payments current account increasing. Spain also has a greater presence in international institutions with a number of posts, including Secretary-General of Nato, Director-General of Unesco, and presidents of the European Parliament, the Western European Union Assembly and the European Court of Justice (ECJ).

## The Relationship between Community Law and Spanish Internal Law

According to Merino Merchán *et al.* (1995), the characteristics of the relationship between European law and internal law include autonomy of Community law against the national law, being a legal system in its own right; and the European law being a complementary legal system for the member states, and a primary system which is imposed on the member states.

The adhesion of Spain to the European treaties has caused complications for the principle of supremacy of the constitution as much as for the system of sources of law. Indeed, the commission's acceptance on 31 May 1985 of Spain's adhesion includes the statement that the states entering the Community accept unreservedly the treaties and their political aims, the decisions adopted from entry into force of the treaties and the primacy of Community law over those national provisions which are contrary, as well as the existence of procedures to ensure uniformity of interpretation of Community law.

The relationship between Community law and Spanish law brings into focus the hierarchy of norms within the Spanish legal system and concerns the autonomous communities as much as the central state. The hierarchy of legal sources which is set out in the Spanish Civil Code includes international treaties. The constitution also includes a chapter on international treaties.

### Article 93 of the Spanish Constitution

Article 93 of the constitution provides for the exercise of certain competences within the national territory to be transferred to the Community organs. The combination of Articles 93 and 96 of the constitution allows European Community law to be integrated into the Spanish legal system. According to Jorge Esteban and González-Trevijano (1992), there are two potential problems which arise from integrating the international treaties into Spanish domestic law: the problem of achieving immediate application of treaty provisions and to what extent this is possible, and the problem of primacy of international law over Spanish internal law.

Article 93 of the constitution was drafted with a view to Spain's entry into the Community so that a clash of principles between Community law and internal law could be avoided. Thus Article 93 provides that a *ley orgánica* would authorize the creation of international treaties by which an international organization or institution would be granted competences derived from the constitution. Spain's entry into the European Community indicated acceptance of Community law as a whole, thereby submitting her legal system to all the demands of the system of Community law.

The constitutional court (Case 28/1991, 14 February) stated that Article 93 has three aspects:

a) the creation of a specified type of international treaty shall only be authorized by a *ley orgánica*;

b) the relevant treaties are those by which are attributed to an international organization or institution any powers derived from the constitution, and

c) the guarantee of compliance with such treaties and the resolutions made by the international organization or institution shall be the responsibility of the *Cortes Generales* or the government.

Spanish law recognizes a distinction between primary Community law sources and secondary sources. The primary sources are the treaties, their annexes and amendments and such primary sources are binding on member states as signatories and individuals. Therefore citizens may seek to enforce the primary laws and argue them before the domestic courts. This arises partly as a result of the jurisprudence of the ECJ and also as a result of the provisions in Articles 93 and 96 of the constitution. Article 93 guarantees compliance with the treaties by the government and parliament and Article 96 states that, once signed and officially published in Spain, the treaty becomes part of the internal law.

The secondary sources of European Community law include regulations, directives and decisions, which are all binding. Recommendations and opinions are not legally binding according to Article 190 of the Treaty of European Union, but Article 93 of the constitution states that, in all cases, the resolutions created by the international or supranational organs or bodies must be complied with by the Spanish government and parliament. Therefore, even those secondary sources form part of the internal law and become immediately applicable. Thus, regardless of the form which they take, resolutions created at Community level become a part of the Spanish domestic law and are immediately applicable. Logically, this leads to the principle of supremacy of European law over Spanish domestic law.

There are a number of reasons for the supremacy of European law in Spain. First, the nature of adhesion to the European treaties involves accepting principles and receiving them into Spain's own legal system. This entails acceptance of a restricted sovereignty in some matters because the community guides the principle of uniform application in all member states. Second, Articles 93 and 96 have the effect of giving supremacy to European Community law. Third, the rulings of the ECJ (such as in the *Simmenthal* case – case 106/77 [1978] ECR 629) lead towards European law's supremacy. Fourth, in the nature of the adhesion to the Community treaties, from the moment of signing the treaty, a series of principles are being accepted and received into the internal legal order. Fifth, the Community is not limited in time. Sixth, member states, by signing the EC Treaty, are accepting a restriction over their own sovereignty in certain matters. Seventh, the Community operates on a principle of uniform application in all member states and also the obligations at community level are unconditional. Another reason is that inferences can be drawn from the Spanish Constitution itself as to the primacy of Community law. For example, Article 93 provides that compliance with what is emanated from the supranational organs will be guaranteed.

Following the requirement in the constitution of a *ley orgánica* for bringing international laws into domestic law, the Law of the Bases for Delegation to the Government for the Application of the Laws of the EC entered into force on 27 December 1985.

It has been made clear that, once created, the Community law becomes part of Spanish law, but what is its status relative to other Spanish laws or rules? Should Community law be applied in preference to the other Spanish provisions? Esteban and González-Trevijano (1992) state that Article 5 of the Treaty of Rome requires that national judicial bodies should apply Community law instead of any contradictory national law. The judge may ask for an opinion by the constitutional court of the constitutionality of the domestic provision or can by his or her own authority leave unapplied the domestic law and prefer the Community law.

One question is whether the constitution has any superiority over Community law. An answer to this question is that Community law is part of the constitution, and where there is a clash Article 95 states the need to alter the constitution in the first place and, finally, where certain powers are transferred to the Community institutions and organizations, this gives supremacy to the Community. Such competences are, however, limited by the constitution. Effectively, the constitution becomes like a species of autonomous statute. The more expansive the powers of the Community become, the more progressively weakened are the powers of each individual state.

As was noted above, the constitution, including Article 93, was drafted with a view to Spain's joining the Community. Therefore Article 93 aimed to avoid the need for constitutional reform on the entry into the EC. Signing the European Treaty means handing over to the Community certain powers, thus giving to the Community a certain level of supremacy. That does not mean to say that the Spanish Constitution may no longer be regarded as a supreme law. It establishes a number of fundamental principles. First, the alteration of the rules relating to attribution of competences arises from the same constitution. Secondly, the introduction into national law of Community law has been made according to the procedure of a *ley orgánica*. Thirdly, the principle of hierarchy has not been put aside but what has been put into operation as well is the principle of competence. Fourthly, the attribution of competences is guided by the constitution, and, fifthly, the transfer of competences cannot result in undermining the constitution because any stipulations made which are contrary to the constitution will require, according to Article 95, a prior constitutional reform.

The increasing moves towards integration have heightened the strength of Community law against the domestic laws of the member states. For Spanish legal theorists, this means that Community law enjoys more supremacy in practice. For example, as a result of the increasing moves towards majority voting, it is possible for a law to be imposed on the Spanish legal system against or contrary to existing Spanish laws, but Spain cannot legislate against the Community laws. This has an effect on the system of hierarchy of laws and it also leads to a system of shared competences and shared supremacy between the Community institutions and the different member states.

According to Villaamil *et al.* (1997), the theory that the European community law's supremacy arises from provisions in the constitution needs to be corrected. The principle of supremacy of Community law requires a wide interpretation of the constitution which favours Community law in order to avoid conflicts between that law and the principles which guide the internal system of sources of law. The constitution was drafted around the same time that the Spanish government had applied for membership of the European Community, in 1977. Thus Article 93 was drafted so as to avoid clashes between Spanish law and Community law. The 1985 law which was established in compliance with Article 93 allowed the adhesion of Spain to the Community to have the effect of Spain accepting Community law in its entirety and submitting its own legal system to the requirements of the Community's legal system.

International treaties have the status of a directly applicable legal rule. If the treaties contain provisions which are contrary to the constitution, they require for their approval prior constitutional reform, and the government as well as either chamber of the *Cortes Generales* may ask the constitutional court to declare if that treaty is or is not compatible with the constitution under Article 95.1 After such a declaration, the international treaty becomes part of the Spanish law through its publication in the Official State Bulletin according to Article 96.1 of the constitution and Article 1.5 of the Civil Code. Article 94.1 of the constitution requires authorization of the *Cortes* so that the state can give its consent to specific types of international treaty. These types of treaty include treaties of a political and military character; treaties which affect the territorial structure of the state, or the fundamental rights and duties provided by the constitution; treaties which imply financial obligations for the state budget; and treaties which require modification or derogation of any law or which demand legislative means for its execution. This authorization is granted by a *ley ordinaria*, for which a simple majority of both houses suffices.

The Treaty of European Union has provoked a conflict between Spanish constitutional law and Community law since the constitutional court has interpreted Article 93 far more strictly than was intended by its drafters. The constitutional court suggests that the constitution enjoys supremacy because a treaty which contradicts it requires the constitution to be altered before the treaty is accepted into the Spanish legal system. If the constitution is not amended then the treaty has no constitutional validity within the Spanish legal system.

The Treaty of European Union was regarded as a contradiction of Article 13.2 of the constitution, which guarantees the right of passive suffrage of community nationals in municipal elections. This required a reform of Article 13.2. In the event, this proved possible, but the fact that this was deemed necessary demonstrates the potential problems if such reform could not occur. Thus what is notable is the restrictive interpretation of the Spanish constitutional court towards the relationship between domestic law and Community law. However, Article 93 seems to be universally recognized as the article which makes possible the integration of Spain and the European Community.

Zapata prefers to regard the relationship between Spanish law and Community law as one of a division of powers rather than as a hierarchy. Furthermore, what is more important from a Community law perspective is that Community law is given practical effect so that some degree of uniformity is achieved and that Community laws cannot be derogated from by later internal laws.

## The Adhesion of Spain to the European Community and the Competences of the Autonomous Communities

The negotiations for Spain's entry into the European Community coincided with the process of the development of autonomy. The process of decentralization was under way when Spain joined the European Community. This process was not to be neutralized by the attribution of constitutional powers to the Community institutions. The Spanish Constitution guarantees to the regions and nationalities in Spain the right to autonomy. When Spain acceded to the Community, all the autonomous communities except Ceuta and Melilla had been established, and each different community had assumed certain competences under the constitution. The competences assumed at Community level were required to follow a similar route.

One problem is that at Community level, the European Council of Ministers is composed of state representatives. Furthermore, the Community laws are required to be applied at state level. This leads to the need for the state to stipulate a requirement for the various autonomous communities to give effect to the European laws. Another problem is that the central state may deal with issues affected by Community measures which are really in the autonomous communities' domain. This may result in the central state acting to the detriment of the autonomous communities. A further problem is the lack of representation of the autonomous communities in the elaboration of Community laws. Perhaps with the exception of the Basque region and Cataluña, the autonomous communities have not had an adequate opportunity to participate in the creation and implementation of Community laws.

The entry of Spain into the Community has meant that, not only have some of the central government's competences been passed to the Community institutions, but also some of the powers of the autonomous communities have transferred to the European level. The state must also guarantee compliance with European laws following Article 93 of the Constitution and so a relevant issue is that of the controls imposed by the state on the autonomous communities to ensure such compliance. Connected with this issue is the effect of Article 149.1.3 of the constitution, which states that matters of international relations are matters reserved for central government. However, Alegre Martínez (1994) suggests that the combined Articles 93 and 149.1.3 should be interpreted to mean that what is transferred is the exercise of certain powers both central and local but these do not give rise to a specific area in which the application or development of Community law corresponds only to central authorities.

Effectively, exclusive competence of the central government with regard to international relations refers to external relations but not necessarily to the application of rules internally. In that case the distribution of powers between central and local government must still be recognized. The popular view remains that adhesion does not alter the share of competences exercised in accordance with the constitution. The sharing of powers is an internal law question so that the appropiate entity for executing the Community law is to be determined by the rules that regulate power sharing. The constitutional court suggests that the state should create basic legislation but this may be developed by the autonomous communities.

The central government may still exercise control over the way in which the autonomous communities react to European laws. The state has obligations under the constitution to comply with the European laws and this includes making sure that at a local level those laws are given effect. This is achieved by a group of governmental, legislative and judicial controls and guarantees. Thus governmental guarantees are exercised in three ways:

through administrative action, through the state being able to prevent provisions or resolutions of the autonomous communities from having effect, and by enforcement mechanisms. Legislative measures may also be adopted in order to fill any gaps left by the laws of the autonomous communities. In that way, Article 149.3 states that the central government may supplement the laws of the autonomous communities. In addition, under Article 150.3, it is possible to harmonize the laws of the different autonomous communities where the public interest demands this. Judicial guarantees mean that the courts situated in the autonomous communities as well as the constitutional court will apply Community law.

The extent to which the autonomous communities are able to participate in the adoption of Community laws and decisions may at first sight appear to be minimal since Article 149.1.3 states that international relations are reserved for the central government. However, a number of the statutes of autonomy require the autonomous communities to be informed of developments of treaties and conventions where those will be relevant to their interests. For example, the statute for the Canary Islands allows that autonomous community to give an opinion on developments.

The Treaty of Maastricht highlighted the special position of the regions and, following that Treaty, the committee of the regions was established. However, in reality, the role of this committee in providing decentralized entities with the opportunity of participating in the creation of certain European laws still needs to be developed.

### References and Further Reading

Alzaga Villaamil, Oscar, Gutiérrez Gutiérrez, Ignacio and Rodríguez Zapata, Jorge, *Derecho Político Español Según La Constitución De 1978* (1997, Editorial Centro de Estudios, Madrid).

Aragón, Manuel, 'La Constitución Española y El Tratado de La Unión Europea: La Reforma de la Constitución' (1994) 14 *Revista Española de Derecho Constitucional*, 9.

de Esteban Jorge and González-Trevijano, Pedro J., *Curso de Derecho Constitucional Español* (1992, Agisa, Madrid).

Featherstone, Kevin, 'The Mediterranean Challenge: cohesion and external preferences', in Juliet Lodge (ed.), *The European Community and the Challenge of the Future* (1989, Pinter, London), p.186.

Heywood, Paul, *The Government and Politics of Spain*, (1996, Macmillan, London).

Martínez, Alegre and Angel, Miguel, 'Comunidades Antónomas y Derecho Communitario Europeo' (1994), *Revista de la Facultad de Derecho de la Universidad Complutense*, pp.277–86.

Merino Merchán, José Fernando *et al.*, *Lecciones de Derecho Constitucional* (1995, Tecnos, Madrid).

Nicholson, Frances and East, Roger *From the Six to the Twelve: The Enlargement of the European Communities* (1987, Longman: London).

Ordóñez Solís, David, *La Ejecución del Derecho Comunitario Europeo en España* (1993, Civitas, Madrid).

Preston, Paul and Smyth, Denis, *Spain, the EEC and NATO* (1984, Routledge & Kegan Paul, London).

Santaolalla Gadea, Francisco, 'La Aplicación del Derecho Comunitario en España' (1984) 201 *Documentación Administrativa*, 83.

Tsoukalis, Loukas, *The European Community and its Mediterranean Enlargement* (1981, Allen & Unwin, London), pp.144–5.

White, David, 'Success without popularity', *Financial Times*, 20 January 1997.

White, David, 'Shadows from past tarnish bright prospects', *Financial Times*, 27 May 1997.

# 12   Conclusion

This book has concentrated mainly on the constitutional aspects of the Spanish law and legal system. This is a deliberate focus since it has been observed that the Civil Code recognizes the constitution as the supreme norm in the hierarchy of legal rules. From this perspective, knowledge of the Spanish Constitution is critical for an understanding of the Spanish legal system because the constitution provides the fundamental principles from which the laws of more specific areas are developed. A knowledge of the constitution also helps to foster an understanding of Spain's political system and the constitution is itself a reflection of Spain's long struggle to achieve democracy.

The fact that Spain has a written constitution at once distinguishes her legal system from that of the UK. Spain follows much more the 'continental' style of legal practice. The existence of a written constitution for Spain has a number of positive consequences. In truth, it would not be unusual to meet a person on the street in Spain who knows at least of the existence of his or her constitutional rights, if not the details. The constitution is easily available in published form and provides a starting point for establishing the legal position in any given situation. However, the major criticism of the constitution is that it is a vague document. For example, not all the rights within the constitution are clearly defined and not all the principles have legally binding force, but instead they provide guidelines for governmental policy. This might be expected in a primary document from which other, more specific, legal rules will be developed. It is also a reflection, however, of the compromise which was necessary at the political level in order to achieve the creation of the constitution.

Part of the compromise which is evident in the constitution relates to the regional organization of Spain. In this aspect Spain is unique. The territorial structure achieved reflects a compromise between the left-wing forces who sought a federalist state structure and the right wing who wanted to retain a centralist state. Thus Spain is not a federal state like Germany; rather, she regards herself as a unified state with a degree of autonomy for the regions. This autonomy is secondary to the principle of unity. Therefore an autonomous community may create its own laws, but these laws must not be antagonistic to the needs of the state at a general level or to general legal principles set out in the constitution. Spain's regional organization may well be of interest to British lawyers as the UK embarks on a devolved Scottish Parliament and assemblies for Wales and Northern Ireland.

Another noteworthy aspect of the constitution is that the procedure for constitutional reform is extremely complex. This complex procedure appears to have deterred efforts to modify the constitution. The alternative approach has been to define the constitutional concepts rather broadly. Thus, for example, by contrast with the experience of France and Italy, the Spanish Constitution has not required modification in order to bring about the privatization of public sector industries such as electricity or telecommunications. This may be because the right of freedom of enterprise which is set out in Article 38 can be read in combination with Article 128, which states that the public sector has a right of economic initiative, with public bodies having precedence for carrying out essential services and monopolies, but that private enterprises might participate where this is in the public interest.

Another aspect of Spanish law which is different from that of the UK is that Spain has a codified system of law. In Spain there exist the Civil Code, the Criminal Code and the Commercial Code. These are all important sources of law setting out the basic principles which are developed by various laws on specific aspects. The Civil Code also sets out the hierarchy of laws within the Spanish legal system. One consequence of this codified system is that case law tends to be interpretative rather than to act as a positive legal precedent, as in English law. The Civil and Commercial Codes date back to the late nineteenth century. The age of these codes causes problems, since it necessitates a large number of supplementary rules, making the civil law and commercial laws more complex still. For example, the rules relating to delictual obligations in the Civil Code are outdated and do not accommodate the needs of a modern, industrialized society. Consequently, a range of specific laws have been created to enable the victim of harm caused by negligence to claim compensation more easily. The Criminal Code, on the other hand, was, after much debate and many drafts, brought up to date, with a new code introduced in 1995. This comprehensive code reflects modern society with the inclusion of crimes such as abuse of genetic modification.

Perhaps a distinctive aspect of the civil law is that a number of regions have their own laws, particularly in the area of property ownership and hereditary succession. These laws are known as foral laws and exist by reason of recognition of the historical positions of those regions which may retain their own laws.

Finally, Spain's entry into the European Community is worthy of note. Spain encountered long and difficult negotiations for entry and it is fair to say that, unlike the UK, which was able to lay down conditions on the Community as part of her negotiations, Spain had to accept conditions imposed on her by the European Community in order to gain entry. This fact may have encouraged a degree of resentment towards Europe, particularly in rural, agricultural areas of Spain. However, it is also evident that Spain has made considerable economic gains since her entry. She has become an influential European Community member and it is notable that, on the world political stage, Spain plays an important role. Within Spain's legal system, European law is undoubtedly given a place of special importance. The constitution, which pre-dated Spain's entry into the Community, was drafted with Europe in mind. Articles 93 and 96 have the effect of giving supremacy to European Community law.

In turn, this has implications for the relationship between the state and the regions, since the autonomous communities will be affected by European law. At the European level, recognition of regional issues has acquired increased importance. Within Spain the level of involvement of the autonomous communities in the process of negotiation of European laws is variable, in part depending on the extent to which each statute of autonomy demands that the state informs that community of developments of relevant treaties and conventions. This is clearly an aspect of Spanish law that requires further consideration for improvement.

There are likely to be plenty of future developments in Spanish law. It is worth highlighting what some of these might be. First, Spain will have to continue to implement any European legal provisions. Perhaps more dramatically, Spain's entry into the Single Monetary Union will certainly have an impact. In France, entry will require reform of the constitution. It is unclear whether this will be necessary in Spain, though it might be argued that the broad scope of Article 93, which transfers to the European Union the exercise of the state's powers, will render such modification of the constitution unnecessary. Another important development may be the achievement of a peace settlement with the Basque region. This process appears to have begun partly as a result of the influence of the peace process which continues in Great Britain with Northern Ireland. This is very much a political process, but it may also carry with it a number of legal implications depending on the outcome of the terms of any such peace agreement. In any event there is clear evidence in Spain of a movement towards decentralization. This trend may in part have been influenced by a dissatisfaction with the government which grew in the 1990s as a result of a number of financial and political scandals in which senior ministers were charged with corruption. This has also led to moves towards a legally regulated government.

Thus, overall, it is clear that many of Spain's legal developments are very much a reflection of the country's political state of affairs. This is as true of the predicted future legal developments as of the creation of the constitution itself, which today forms the entry point into an understanding of Spain's law and legal system.

# Index

157